The Return of Martin Guerre

The Return of
Martin Guerre

Natalie Zemon Davis

Harvard University Press
Cambridge, Massachusetts
London, England

Library of Congress Cataloging in Publication Data

Davis, Natalie Zemon, 1928–
The return of Martin Guerre.

Bibliography: p.
1. Du Tilh, Arnault, d. 1560.
2. Guerre, Martin.
3. Impostors and imposture—France.   I. Title.
LAW   345.44'0263   83-277
ISBN 0-674-76690-3 (cloth)   344.405263
ISBN 0-674-76691-1 (paper)

Designed by Gwen Frankfeldt

For Chandler Davis

Preface

THIS BOOK GREW out of a historian's adventure with a different way of telling about the past. The story of Martin Guerre has been recounted many times. In the 1540s in Languedoc, a rich peasant leaves his wife, child, and property and is not heard from for years; he comes back—or so everyone thinks—but after three or four years of agreeable marriage the wife says she has been tricked by an impostor and brings him to trial. The man almost persuades the court he is Martin Guerre, when at the last moment the true Martin Guerre appears. Two books were immediately written about the case, one by a judge of the court. All over France there were comments on it, by the great Montaigne among others. Over the centuries it was retold in books on famous impostors and *causes célèbres,* and is still remembered in the Pyrenean village of Artigat where the events took place four hundred years ago. It has inspired a play, two novels, and an operetta.

When I first read the judge's account I thought, "This must become a film." Rarely does a historian find so perfect a narrative structure in the events of the past or one with such dramatic popular appeal. By coincidence I learned that the scenarist Jean-Claude Carrière and the director Daniel

Vigne were starting a screenplay on the same subject. I was able to join them, and out of our collaboration came the film *Le Retour de Martin Guerre.*

Paradoxically, the more I savored the creation of the film, the more my appetite was whetted for something beyond it. I was prompted to dig deeper into the case, to make historical sense of it. Writing for actors rather than readers raised new questions about the motivations of people in the sixteenth century—about, say, whether they cared as much about truth as about property. Watching Gérard Depardieu feel his way into the role of the false Martin Guerre gave me new ways to think about the accomplishment of the real impostor, Arnaud du Tilh. I felt I had my own historical laboratory, generating not proofs, but historical possibilities.

At the same time, the film was departing from the historical record, and I found this troubling. The Basque background of the Guerres was sacrificed; rural Protestantism was ignored; and especially the double game of the wife and the judge's inner contradictions were softened. These changes may have helped to give the film the powerful simplicity that had allowed the Martin Guerre story to become a legend in the first place, but they also made it hard to explain what actually happened. Where was there room in this beautiful and compelling cinematographic recreation of a village for the uncertainties, the "perhapses," the "may-have-beens," to which the historian has recourse when the evidence is inadequate or perplexing? Our film was an exciting suspense story that kept the audience as unsure of the outcome as the original villagers and judges had been. But where was there room to reflect upon the significance of identity in the sixteenth century?

The film thus posed the problem of invention to the historian as surely as it was posed to the wife of Martin Guerre.

I had to return to my original métier; even from location in the Pyrenees I was running off to archives in Foix, Toulouse, and Auch. I would give this arresting tale its first full-scale historical treatment, using every scrap of paper left me by the past. I would figure out why Martin Guerre left his village and where he went, how and why Arnaud du Tilh became an impostor, whether he fooled Bertrande de Rols, and why he failed to make it stick. This would tell us new things about sixteenth-century rural society. I would follow the villagers through the criminal courts and explain the judges' changing verdicts. And I would have the rare opportunity to show an event from peasant life being reshaped into a story by men of letters.

It turned out to be much more difficult than I had thought—but what a pleasure to recount the history of Martin Guerre once again.

N.Z.D.

Princeton
January 1983

Acknowledgments

I am grateful to Princeton University and to the National Endowment for the Humanities for financial assistance in preparing this book. I also want to thank the archivists and staff of the Archives Départementales of the Ariège, the Haute-Garonne, the Gers, the Pyrénées-Atlantiques, the Gironde, and the Pas-de-Calais for their advice and courtesy, which made possible rapid progress in my research. Marie-Rose Bélier, Paul Dumons, and Hubert Daraud of Artigat were willing to share with me their memories of their village and of the story of Martin Guerre. Jean-Claude Carrière and Daniel Vigne gave me new ways to think about the connections between the "general trends" of historians and the living experience of the people. Emmanuel Le Roy Ladurie provided important encouragement when it was needed. Ideas and bibliographical suggestions were offered by numerous colleagues in the United States and France: Paul Alpers, Yves and Nicole Castan, Barbara B. Davis, William A. Douglass, Daniel Fabre, Stephen Greenblatt, Richard Helmholz, Paul Hiltpold, Elizabeth Labrousse, Helen Nader, Laurie Nussdorfer, Jean-Pierre Poussou, Virginia Reinburg, and Ann Waltner. Alfred Soman was generous in his advice for the chapters on criminal justice. The editing of Joyce Backman added much to the clarity of the the text. Without the help of my authentic husband, Chandler Davis, this history of an impostor-spouse could never have existed.

Contents

Illustrations

....•————◀◈▶————•....

ARREST ME-
MORABLE, DV PAR-
LEMENT DE
TOLOSE,

Contenant vne histoire prodigieuse, de
nostre temps, auec cent belles, & doctes Annotations, de monsieur maistre IEAN DE CORAS, Conseiller
en ladite Cour, & rapporteur du
proces.

Prononcé es Arrestz Generaulx le xij.
Septembre M. D. LX.

A Raison cede.

VIN
CEN
TI.

A LYON,
PAR ANTOINE VINCENT,
M. D. LXI.
Auec Priuilege du Roy.

Claudij Puteanj

ARREST DV PARLEMENT

de Tolose, contenant vne histoire memorable,
& prodigieuse, auec cent belles & doctes
Annotations, de monsieur maistre
IEAN DE CORAS, rap-
porteur du proces.

Texte de la toile du proces
& de l'arrest.

V moys de Ianuier, mil
cinq cens cinquante neuf,
Bertrande de Rolz, du lieu
d'Artigat , au diocese de
Rieux , se rend suppliant,
& plaintiue, deuant le Iu-
ge de Rieux : disant , que
vingt ans peuuët estre pas-
sez, ou enuiron, qu'elle estant ieune fille , de neuf à
dix ans, fut mariee, auec Martin Guerre, pour lors
aussi fort ieune, & presque de mesmes aage, que
la suppliant.

Annotation I.

Les mariages ainsi contractez auant l'aage legitime , ordonné
de nature, ou par les loix politiques, ne peuuent estre (s'il est loy-
sible de sonder , iusques aux secretz , & inscrutables iugemens de
la diuinité)plaisans, ny aggreables à Dieu, & l'issue, en est le plus
souuent piteuse,& miserable, & (comme on voit iournellement
par exemple) pleine, de mille repentances : par tant qu'en telles
precoces , & deuancees conionctions, ceux qui ont tramé, & au titre de fri-
proietté le tout , n'ont aucunement respecté l'honneur , & la gid & malefic.
gloire de Dieu:& moins la fin , pour laquelle ce saint , & venera- de vot. & vot.
ble estat de mariage , ha esté par luy institué du commencement iesme.
du monde. ᵃ (qui fut deuant l'offence de nostre premier pere,
pour

a chap.dernier
au titre de fri-
gid.& malefic.
aux Decreta-
les & au ch.vn.
de vot. & vot.
redemp.au Six
iesme.

Introduction

····•──◄◆►──•····

"FEMME BONNE qui a mauvais mary, a bien souvent le coeur marry" (A good wife with a bad husband often has a sorry heart). "Amour peut moult, argent peut tout" (love may do much, but money more). These are some of the sayings by which peasants characterized marriage in sixteenth-century France.[1] Historians have been learning more and more about rural families from marriage contracts and testaments, from parish records of births and deaths, and from accounts of courtship rituals and charivaris.[2] But we still know rather little about the peasants' hopes and feelings; the ways in which they experienced the relation between husband and wife, parent and child; the ways in which they experienced the constraints and possibilities in their lives. We often think of peasants as not having had much in the way of choices, but is this in fact true? Did individual villagers ever try to fashion their lives in unusual and unexpected ways?

But how do historians discover such things about anyone in the past? We look at letters and diaries, autobiographies, memoirs, family histories. We look at literary sources—plays, lyric poems, and stories—which, whatever their relation to the real lives of specific people, show us what sentiments and reactions authors considered plausible for a given period. Now the peasants, more than ninety percent of whom could not write in the sixteenth century, have left us few documents of self-revelation. The family histories and journals that have come down to us from them are sparse: an entry or two on births and deaths and the weather. Thomas Platter can give us a portrait of his hard-working peasant mother: "Except one time when we said good-bye to her, I never saw my mother cry; she was a courageous and virile woman, but rough." But this was written when that learned Hebraist had long since left his Swiss village and mountain pastures behind him.[3]

As for literary sources on the peasants, where they exist, they follow the classical rules that make villagers a subject of comedy. Comedy is about "personnes populaires," people of low condition, so the theory went. "In a style humble and low, comedy represents the private fortunes of men . . . Its issue is happy, pleasant, and agreeable." So in *Les Cent Nouvelles Nouvelles* (the fifteenth-century collection of comic stories, several times reprinted in the sixteenth century), an acquisitive peasant comes upon his wife having sexual intercourse with a friend, is mollified in his rage by the promise of twelve measures of grain, and then to keep the bargain has to let the lovers finish up. In the *Propos Rustiques*, published by the Breton lawyer Noël du Fail in 1547, the old peasant Lubin reminisces about when he got married at the age of thirty-four: "I hardly knew what it was to be in love . . . but nowadays there is hardly a young man past fifteen who hasn't tried something out with the girls."[4] The image of peasant feeling and behavior that emerges from such accounts is not without its value—comedy is, after all, an important way to explore the human condition—but it is limited in its psychological register and in the range of situations in which villagers are placed.

But there exists another set of sources in which peasants are found in many predicaments and in which the ending is not always happy: the records of different court jurisdictions. It is to the registers of the Inquisition that we owe Emmanuel Le Roy Ladurie's picture of the Cathar village of Montaillou and Carlo Ginzburg's study of the daring miller Menocchio. The records of diocesan courts are full of marriage cases, which historians have been using to understand how villagers and cityfolk maneuvered within the tight world of custom and law to find a suitable mate.[5]

And then there are the records of various criminal jurisdictions. Here, for instance, is the story told in 1535 to the king by a young Lyonnais villager who was trying to win a pardon for an impulsive murder. Even allowing for the phrases urged upon him by his attorney or notary, we have a portrait of an unhappy marriage:

> About a year ago the said suppliant, having found a partner with a good dowry, married Ancely Learin and since then supported her honestly as his wife and sought to live with her in peace. But the said Ancely, without rhyme or reason, took it into her head to kill him, and in fact beat him and threw stones at him ... The suppliant accepted this peaceably, thinking things would calm down after a time ... But then one Sunday earlier this month of May, he was quietly eating with her and asked her for a drink of wine. She said she would give it to him in the head, threw the bottle at him and spilled wine all over his face ... Then in her fury, she picked up a tureen and would have wounded the suppliant seriously if the servant-girl had not put herself between them ... Being very excited, he picked up a bread knife, ran after the said Ancely and stuck it in her stomach.

The wife did not live long enough to tell her side of the story.[6]

From such documents we learn of peasant expectations and feelings at a time of sudden agitation or crisis. In 1560, however, there came before the Parlement of Toulouse a criminal case that revealed peasant marriages over many years, a case so extraordinary that one of the men who judged it published a book about it. His name was Jean de Coras, a native of the region, distinguished doctor of laws, author of Latin commentaries on the civil and canon law and humanist. Coras's *Arrest Memorable* summed up all the evidence, formal arguments, and judgments in the case and included his annotations upon them. It was not a comedy, he said, but a tragedy, even though the actors were rustics, "people of low condition." Written in French, the book was reprinted five times in the next six years and had several more editions in French and Latin before the end of the century.[7]

Combining features of a legal text and a literary tale, Coras's book on the case of Martin Guerre leads us into the hidden world of peasant sentiment and aspiration. That it is an unusual case serves me well, for a remarkable dispute can sometimes uncover motivations and values that are lost in the welter of the everyday. My hope is to show that the adventures of three young villagers are not too many steps beyond the more common experience of their neighbors, that an impostor's fabrication has links with more ordinary ways of creating personal identity. I also want to explain why a story that seemed fit for a mere popular pamphlet—and indeed was told in that form—became in addition the subject for a judge's "one hundred and eleven beautiful annotations"; and to suggest why we have here a rare identification between the fate of peasants and the fate of the rich and learned.

For sources I start with Coras's *Arrest* of 1561 and the short *Historia* of Guillaume Le Sueur, published the same

year. The latter is an independent text, dedicated to another
judge in the case; in at least two instances, it has material
not found in Coras but which I have verified in archival
sources.[8] I use Le Sueur and Coras to supplement each
other, though in the few places where they are in conflict I
give greater weight to the judge. In the absence of the full
testimony from the trial (all such records for criminal cases
before 1600 are missing for the Parlement of Toulouse), I
have worked through the registers of Parlementary sentences to find out more about the affair and about the practice and attitudes of the judges. In pursuit of my rural
actors, I have searched through notarial contracts in villages
all over the dioceses of Rieux and Lombez. When I could
not find my individual man or woman in Hendaye, in Artigat, in Sajas, or in Burgos, then I did my best through other
sources from the period and place to discover the world they
would have seen and the reactions they might have had.
What I offer you here is in part my invention, but held
tightly in check by the voices of the past.

I

From Hendaye to Artigat

····•——◄◆►——•····

IN 1527 the peasant Sanxi Daguerre, his wife, his young
son Martin, and his brother Pierre left the family property in the French Basque country and moved to a village in
the county of Foix, a three-week walk away.

It was not the most usual thing for a Basque to do. Not
that the men of Labourd were stay-at-homes, but when they
traveled it was more likely out to sea, to trap whales on the
Atlantic, even as far as Labrador. When they left for good,
they were more likely to cross the Bidassoa River into the
Spanish Basque country or down into Spain, rather than
turn inland north of the Pyrenees. And the men who
moved away were usually not heir to their family's property,
as was Sanxi Daguerre, but younger brothers who could not
or would not remain in the ancestral household. So important were these family houses to Basque villagers that each
was given a name which the heir and his wife assumed:
"They call themselves Lords and Ladies of such-and-such a
house, even if it is only a pigpen," a hostile observer was to
claim later on.[1]

Sanxi Daguerre's house was no pigpen, however. It was
located in Hendaye, right on the border between France and
Spain, a village of few houses, according to a traveler in

1528, but with extensive common lands. Living between the mountains, the river, and the ocean, the villagers herded sheep, fished, and farmed. The clay soil was not much good for grains other than millet, but was excellent for apple trees; the Daguerre brothers used the clay to develop a sideline in tilemaking. Life was not easy in the Labourd, but it had its strong points, at least in the eyes of some visitors: they note the beauty of the villages; the wonder and danger of the offshore whale hunt and the dividing of the catch; the men, women, and children playing in the waves. "Throughout this country, the people are gay ... they are always laughing, joking and dancing, women and men both," went one comment in 1528.[2]

Nevertheless, Sanxi Daguerre decided to leave. Perhaps it was the continual threat of warfare in the region; the Basque country and Navarre were long sources of dispute between France and Spain, and the conflicts between François I and the emperor Charles V had their consequences for this frontier area. In 1523 the imperial troops swept through Hendaye and ravaged the Labourd; in 1524 the plague hit especially hard; in 1525 Sanxi's first child Martin was born. Perhaps it was something personal, a quarrel between Sanxi and his father, the senior "lord of the household" (the *senior echekojaun*, as he was called in Basque), if he were still alive, or with some other person. Perhaps Martin's mother had urged the move, for the Basque women were said to be forward, making known their wants.[3]

Whatever the cause, Sanxi packed up his belongings and departed with his family and his younger unmarried brother. The ancestral property would remain in Hendaye, and one day Martin would inherit it. Sanxi could not have sold it easily even if he had wanted to, for the Fors—that is, the customs of the Labourd—prohibited the alienation of patrimonial goods except in cases of dire necessity and then only with the consent of other interested kin.[4] He was free to dispose of his *acquêts*—whatever he had acquired by his own industry—and Sanxi took with him enough resources to get himself well established in his new village.

The roads the family traveled on its trek east were busy ones. They crossed a region of age-old trade exchange between the Pyrenees and the plains, its economy now quickening as Toulouse intensified its role as a major center of redistribution.[5] Between the Save River and the Ariège River, the boundaries that would be important in their new life, moved carts of pastel balls, on their way to the Toulouse dyeing shops; fleece, woolens rough and fine, wood, grain, wine, and fruit. The Daguerres would have seen merchants and peddlers going to local fairs and markets; herdsmen taking sheep and cattle up to the mountains for the summer or down as far as the plains of Toulouse and Pamiers for the winter; pilgrims finding their way to the still popular shrine of Saint James of Compostela; and the young men leaving their villages behind them for the streets of Toulouse and elsewhere. At last the family stopped at Artigat, a village located in the large plain below the foothills of the Pyrenees, a few hours' ride by horse from Pamiers.

Artigat stretched out on either side of the Lèze, a small river compared to the Ariège to the east and the Garonne to the west, but still turbulent enough to overflow its banks from time to time and devastate the peasants' lands. On these lands and on the hills just above them lived some sixty or seventy families, growing the millet well known to Sanxi and Pierre Daguerre but also wheat, oats, and grape vines, and pasturing cows, goats, and especially sheep. A few

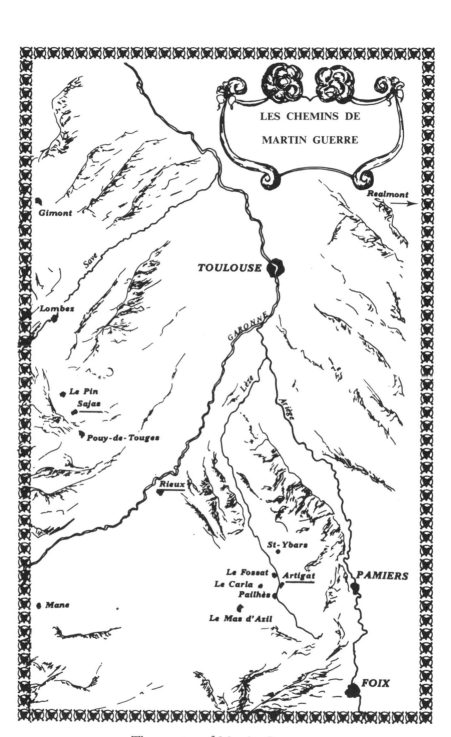

The routes of Martin Guerre

artisans worked in Artigat—a blacksmith, a miller, a shoe-maker, and a dressmaker; perhaps there was some weaving as there surely was at the nearby burg of Le Fossat. Market days were held from time to time and members of the Ban-quels family even referred to themselves as "merchants," but the medieval fairs at Artigat were gone and most local com-merce now went on at Le Fossat. Artigat did have a resident notary by 1562, and perhaps earlier, but in any case a notary from Le Fossat made the rounds to write down contracts in the village houses.[6]

The economic link of Artigat with nearby villages and burgs would have been apparent to the Daguerres at once. Most important was the back-and-forth among Artigat and the village of Pailhès just upstream, Le Fossat just down-stream, and the burg of Le Carla up on a hill to the west. Exchange could also take one down the Lèze as far as Saint-Ybars, east over to the city of Pamiers, and back toward the Pyrenees to Le Mas-d'Azil. Jean Banquels of Artigat rents a mare for six years to a peasant from Pailhès. A merchant from Le Fossat rents oxen to two farmers from Le Carla, who will pay him with grain later at the September fair in Pamiers. Jehannot Drot of Artigat goes to Le Fossat every winter to contract for the sale of the fleece from his Spanish sheep; he is paid at once and will return with the wool in May. Others sell their fleece to merchants in Pamiers. A shepherd from Le Carla makes an agreement of *gasailhe* (as it is called in the langue d'oc) with a merchant of Saint-Ybars: he is granted thirty ewes, which he will feed and pasture at his expense; merchant and shepherd will share the cost of his taking them "up to the mountain" and will split the profits half and half. James Loze of Pailhès has a partner-ship with a merchant of Pamiers for fifty-two ewes; they share expenses and profits, wool going to Pamiers after shearing and salt going to Pailhès. Grains and wines move also, either in the form of rents paid in kind or as purchases made by peasants at Le Fossat and Pamiers.[7]

Such a busy little world could not have seemed totally alien to the Daguerres, for there was also exchange among villages and burgs in the Labourd. What was really different from the Basque country was the way the land moved, both in inheritance and in sales. Here in the plain below the Pyrenees there was very little effort among the common people to hold the family property together. The testaments in the area around Artigat rarely benefit one child but instead provide dowries for the daughters and divide the inheritance equally among the sons, even if there are five of them. (If there are only daughters, the property is divided equally among them.) Sometimes two brothers or brothers-in-law then decide to farm together; sometimes a brother leaves the village and bequeaths his portion to another heir; most often (as we can see by the land register, the *terrier*, of Artigat in the seventeenth century) the heirs divide the land and live near one another. When a household is set up with two generations of married folk, it is not the Basque combination of the old heir and the young heir, but a widowed parent, usually the mother, with one of her married children.[8]

In this situation a piece of inherited property can be sold with much less hindrance than in the Labourd. So a priest of Le Fossat sells a garden to a merchant, explaining he has had to support his old parents for the past eight years. So Antoine Basle of Artigat sells for a modest 35 livres "the fourth part of the goods and succession of late Jacques Basle his father" to a man from a nearby hamlet, and the brothers Caldeyro sell six setérées of their land (a little under three acres) to the brothers Grose of Le Mas-d'Azil, who are taking up residence in Artigat.[9]

That inherited property (*les propres*) was sold from time

to time did not mean that the peasants along the Lèze River were not attached to their lands. Whole sections of the jurisdiction of Artigat had designations that were also family names: "Les Banquels," not far from the village center; "Rols" to the west; "Le Fustié" near the Lèze, where the miller Fustié lived. Plowed fields had names, too, as did vineyards and meadows—"a la plac," "al sobe," "les asempres," "al cathala," "la bardasse"—and peasants who aquired them sometimes took these titles as an alias.[10]

Of course the identification between family and land was limited at Artigat, probably more than it had been at Hendaye, by the social and economic structure of the village. At its top were affluent families, like the Banquels and after them the Rols, who had many parcels of property scattered throughout Artigat, some of which they farmed themselves and some rented out to other families for fixed payments or a share of the crop. These were the men who collected the revenues from the church benefices within Artigat, buying that right every year from the bishop of Rieux, and who directed the parish confraternity at the village church. They hobnobbed with the best families outside the world of the seigniors: the Loze of Pailhès; the Boëri, rural traders and shoemakers of Le Fossat; the Du Fau, notaries at Saint-Ybars. In contrast to this village elite we come across Bernard Bertrand and his wife, who have an inadequate sixteen setérées of land to support themselves and six children; the shepherd Jehannot Drot, who has to borrow wine and grains when times are hard; and the Faure brothers, sharecroppers who are so far behind in their payments that they are brought to court by their proprietor.[11]

None of the inhabitants of Artigat paid manorial dues or owed manorial services to a seignior, however. Whatever lands they had, they held free and allodial, a fact of which they were very proud. For at least a hundred years there had been no noble properties in the village; a certain Jean d'Escornebeuf, seignior of Lanoux just to the west of Artigat, was buying lands there after the Daguerres' arrival, but he had to pay taille on them, just like any peasant. All the administration in the village belonged either to the community itself or to the king, represented in the first instance by his judge at Rieux, a town several hours' ride away, by the sénéchal of Toulouse, and on appeal by the Parlement of Toulouse. On the lowest level were three or four consuls of Artigat, local worthies approved annually by the judge of Rieux to wear the red and white hoods of village office. They had jurisdiction over agricultural matters, such as the common lands (rather small in extent in Artigat) and the date for starting the winter harvest; wardships, inventories, and auctions of goods post-mortem; complaints of false weights and measures; and disruption of public order by blasphemy and petty assaults. From time to time they called assemblies of the male inhabitants.[12]

All of this must have appealed to the Daguerres, who had grown up in an area where (despite the growing power of the "noble" Urtubies) the seigniorial regime had been weak and where all parishoners had the freedom to meet whenever they wished to draw up statutes for their common needs. If the family had settled just upstream at Pailhès, where the Villemurs, seigniors of Pailhès and captains of the Château de Foix, had their castle, it would have been a different story.[13] The case of Martin Guerre might never have run its course if a resident seignior or his agents had had the authority to intervene. As it was, the Artigatois had to deal much of the time only with the gossip and pressure of their peers.

Apart from its distinctive freedoms, Artigat had a rather

fluid, mixed identity. Linguistically, it was right on the border between the differing nasals and liquid sounds of Gascon and langue d'oc. Geographically, it was within the county of Foix, but together with Pailhès and some other villages it fell under the government of Languedoc. Though near Pamiers, the seat of the diocese of Pamiers, Artigat was part of the diocese of the more distant Rieux. The rector of the main parish church, Saint-Sernin of Artigat, was named by the canons of Saint-Etienne, even farther away in Toulouse; the curate of Bajou, a smaller parish that fell within the jurisdiction of Artigat, was also put in place by a chapter in Toulouse. The men of Artigat might move across several boundaries in the course of their activities as farmers, shepherds, litigants, and Christians, and people called them different things; Gascons, "Foixiens," Languedociens.[14]

Into this village, then, came the Daguerres, settling to the east of the Lèze, acquiring land (perhaps buying someone else's *propres*), and establishing a tileworks as they had at Hendaye. The brothers had a joint household, for a time anyway, and they prospered—"they became rather comfortable for people of small estate," as the pamphleteer Guillaume Le Sueur said of them later. Their holdings increased on the hills up toward Bajou, and along with their tiles and bricks, there was now wheat, millet, vines, and sheep.[15]

To be accepted by the village they had to take on some Languedoc ways. Daguerre became Guerre; if Pierre had used the Basque form of his name, Betrisantz or even Petri, he now changed it. Sanxi's wife probably continued to carry baskets of grain on her head, but she restitched her headdress and the decorations on her skirt so as to fit in with her neighbors. At the parish mass, she would have to get used to the fact that here women did not push ahead of the men to make their offerings, did not go about the church to collect for the vestry, and did not serve as sacristans.[16]

And all of them would have become more fluent in the langue d'oc and become accustomed to a world where the written word was used more frequently than at Hendaye. "The language of the Basques," wrote Judge de Coras, "is so obscure and difficult that many have thought that it can not be expressed by any written characters." In fact, an edition of poetry in Basque was printed at Bordeaux in 1545, but what administrative records and contracts there were in the Labourd were kept in Gascon or in French. In their native land the Guerres would have done their business orally in Basque, Spanish, or Gascon. In the area between the Garonne and the Ariège, they often did it before notaries. The latter were scattered about in many small burgs, and even before the royal Edict of Villars-Cotteret of 1539 required it, they drew up contracts in French with occasional words and spellings in Occitan. The Guerres developed enough writing skills to keep simple accounts, though, like most inhabitants of Artigat, they never signed their contracts with their names and they probably could not read. Indeed, there was no schoolmaster at Artigat to teach them to do so.[17]

While they were sinking their roots into the village, their family grew. Sanxi's wife gave birth to more children, and four daughters survived the perils of infancy. Pierre Guerre took a wife of his own, and following the Basque custom in which married brothers ordinarily did not live together, he seems to have moved into a separate house not far from Sanxi's. Some division of properties was presumably made between the brothers as well. And then, in 1538, the Guerres were present at a contract that marked how far they had come in their eleven years in Artigat: the marriage of

Sanxi's only son Martin to Bertrande de Rols, daughter of the well-off Rols family on the other side of the Lèze.

That Bertrande's father thought this an acceptable match bears further witness to the relative openness of the village to newcomers during these years. Another family, the Groses, had moved from Le Mas-d'Azil and were making good, associating with the Banquels and being chosen as consuls. Many marriages were contracted within the jurisdiction of Artigat, sometimes between spouses from each parish as with the Rols and the Guerres, but inevitably some brides or grooms came from farther away. Jeanne de Banquels married Philippe Du Fau from Saint-Ybars, while Arnaud de Bordenave brought in his young wife and her mother from a village in the diocese of Couserans. Though the Basque country was more distant yet, immigrants from that region were not unknown in the diocese of Rieux: over on the Garonne in Palaminy, for example, lived Bernard Guerra and his wife Marie Dabadia, both good Basque names. Perhaps the Guarys of Artigat also came initially from the Labourd.[18]

The spouses in the Rols-Guerre contract were unusually young. The work of historical demographers would have us expect them to be at least in their late teens, but Martin was only in his fourteenth year; and if Bertrande was as young as she later said,* her marriage was illicit by canon law. The Rols and the Guerres were very eager for an alliance, how-

---

*Bertrande said in her complaint to the judge of Rieux that "being a young girl, nine to ten years old, she was married to Martin Guerre, also very young at the time and near to the same age as the suppliant" (Jean de Coras, *Arrest Memorable du Parlement de Tholose* ... [Paris, 1572], p.1). But Martin Guerre was supposed to be thirty-five at the time of the trial in 1560 (Coras, p. 76), and the testimony about the number of years he lived with Bertrande, and the like, makes him close to fourteen at the time of the wedding. Bertrande had probably reached the stage of puberty too.

ever, and the curate of Artigat, Messire Jacques Boëri, was from a local family and evidently put up no obstruction. As Le Sueur was to comment, "thus the hope for some posterity settles in the minds not only of kings but of country folk, and they take care to marry their children in tender years."[19]

Along with future progeny, goods and exchange of service were surely considerations. The Guerre tileworks may have been important to the Rols, and Bertrande's brother important to the Guerres, with all their daughters. The marriage contract of Bertrande and Martin has not survived, but we can assume its content from numerous others that have. Marriage in the area between the Garonne and Ariège was not usually a time for large transfers of land from one peasant family to another; the bulk of the property was kept, as we have seen, to be divided among the sons in *inter vivos* gifts and testaments. Still, daughters were given money for their dowry equivalent to the sale price of, say, a vineyard or a field. In modest households the payment was spread over several years. Affluent families paid it to the new couple all at once, and in a few cases they added a bit of land. The dowry of young Bertrande de Rols was probably of the latter kind: a cash payment of from 50 to 150 livres—a small gift for a city bride but generous by country standards—and a vineyard west of the Lèze called Delbourat. (It was next to other Rols lands and is found among the Guerre holdings later in the sixteenth century.) Beyond this there were the household goods and clothes that came with every bride in the region: a bed with feather pillows, sheets of linen and wool, a bedcover, a coffer with lock and key, and two or three dresses of different hues.[20]

The children were married in the church of Artigat, where Bertrande's grandfather Andreu and other ancestors lay buried. Then a wedding procession went back to the house of Sanxi Guerre, where in Basque fashion the young lord of the household would expect to live with the old. After an evening of banqueting, the couple was escorted to Bertrande's marriage bed. Into their room at midnight burst the young village revelers, led by Catherine Boëri, a relative of the curate of Artigat. She was carrying their *"resveil."* Heavily seasoned with herbs and spices, the drink would ensure the newlyweds ardent mating and a fertile marriage.[21]

2

The Discontented Peasant

....•———◀◆▶———•....

NOTHING HAPPENED in Bertrande's marriage bed, it seemed, neither that night nor for more than eight years afterward. Martin Guerre was impotent; the couple had been "cast under a spell."[1]

That may not have been the first of Martin's misfortunes. Perhaps it was not so easy for the boy from the Labourd to grow up in Artigat. There were languages to sort out: his parents' Basque and their accented languc d'oc and the language spoken by the people he saw at the tileworks, at harvest, and at mass. Sometimes he must have been allowed to play with the village youngsters—their elders complained about the children stealing grapes off the vines—and surely he was teased because of his name, Martin. It was common enough in Hendaye, but strange in those years among the Jehans, Arnauds, Jameses, Andreus, Guilhaumes, Antoines, Peys, and Bernards of Artigat. That it was the name of a nearby parish made no difference. Martin was what the peasants called an animal, an ass, and in local tradition the bear that the shepherds saw up in the mountains.[2]

In the Guerre family, the young lord of the household had to cope not just with one but with two powerful male personalities, both with fiery tempers. Behind him there were nothing but girls, his sister Jeanne and three others, and his cousins, the daughters of Pierre Guerre—nothing but *pisseuses*. Then, when his penis had barely begun to grow behind his codpiece, another girl came into his life, Bertrande de Rols.

It may never have crossed Sanxi Guerre's mind that his son would have trouble consummating the marriage. The union of so young a lad might be thought wrong in the village because he would lack the economic means and the judgment to have a family of his own and because the watery and tender "humors" of his adolescent body might produce weak semen (so people believed in the sixteenth century). But once a boy had his pubic hair, the pricks of the flesh were thought to start naturally; if anything, they were too strong.

For a while Martin and his family might have hoped the impotence would pass. In the Basque country there was a custom that allowed young men "the freedom to try out their women . . . before marrying them"; maybe this could be looked at as a period of sexual trial. But Martin was growing up to be a tall, slender youth, very agile in the way Basque men were supposed to be and good at village swordplay and acrobatics. Bertrande was growing into a beautiful young woman ("*belle*" would be the first word Coras later used to describe her). Still nothing happened. Bertrande's family was pressing her to separate from Martin; since the marriage was unconsummated, it could be dissolved after three years and she would be free by canon law to marry again.[3]

It was humiliating, and the village surely let them know about it. A married couple who had not had a pregnancy after a certain period of time was a perfect target for a charivari, a *caribari* or *calivari*, as it was called in the area around Pamiers. The young men who fenced and boxed with Martin must have darkened their faces, put on women's clothes, and assembled in front of the Guerre house, beating on wine vats, ringing bells, and rattling swords.[4] It was indeed humiliating.

Martin was bewitched. Bertrande said later that the two of them were "tied" by "the charms of a sorceress" so that they could not perform the marriage act—a sorceress jealous of the Guerres and their fine alliance with the Rols or the agent of a jealous man or woman. (Today a husband's impotence is often blamed on the dominance or carping of his wife. In the sixteenth century, it was usually blamed on the power of a woman outside the marriage.) Given the tradition of popular curing both in the Labourd and in the county of Foix, the couple must have consulted a local wise woman more than once. Finally, after some eight years, an old woman "appeared suddenly as if from heaven" and told them how to lift the spell. They had four masses said by priests and were given sacred hosts and special cakes to eat. Martin consummated his marriage; Bertrande conceived immediately, and a son was born and baptized with his grandfather's Basque name Sanxi.[5]

But things were still not well with the new father. If we can judge Martin Guerre's state of mind from how he chose to spend the next twelve years of his life, there was very little he liked about Artigat beyond his swordplay and acrobatics with the other young men. His precarious sexuality after years of impotence, his household of sisters who would soon be marrying, his position as heir, now underscored by the arrival of his son Sanxi, he wanted none of it. At best the relationship between the old landlord and the young landlord was delicate in a Basque household; one can imagine what it was like between the insistent father Sanxi and the reluctant son Martin.

Much of the time historians of population movement

think of peasant migration as due only to economic considerations; the case of the Guerres shows this is not the whole story. Martin dreamed of life beyond the confines of fields of millet, of tileworks, properties, and marriages. He had traveled some: he had been east to Pamiers for his confirmation and undoubtedly on other trips, and he had been west to Mane on the Salat River, where he had made friends with the local hotelkeeper.[6] But everything led back to Artigat. Village society in fact did have institutions that allowed a young man a breathing space, a respectable if temporary release from the constraints of family life. In the Basque country, it was the sea and whaling trips; surely Martin had heard about this from his uncle and his parents. Throughout the Pyrenees and the plain below them, it was the movement of shepherds with their flocks, as Le Roy Ladurie has shown so beautifully for Pierre Maury of Montaillou.[7] The first was not a practical option for a resident of the inland county of Foix; the second was no longer a social option for the best families in Artigat. The men who took sheep "to the mountain" were not held down by the crops, trading, and other business of the Lèze valley.

Could one find other ways to leave? There was a school at Le Fossat; young Dominique Boëri had studied there and would go off to university and become a bachelor of laws. There were the bands and legions of François I, being raised in Languedoc as elsewhere. Back in the Labourd there were Daguerres who had served in the king's army. Even a dignified notary in Le Mas-d'Azil dreamed about it and drew pictures of soldiers in his registers. And there was Spain, luring men every year from the diocese of Rieux. Pey del Rieux from Saint-Ybars, "having made up his mind to go to Spain and earn his living," makes his will before he departs so his sister can have his property if he should die. François Bonecase from Lanoux takes his wife with him to Barcelona, but

there are also marriage contracts in which the groom specifies how the bride will be fed and lodged by his parents if he should decide to go to Spain after the wedding.[8]

None of these were courses to which Sanxi Guerre would have given assent for his son Martin. But then in 1548, when the infant Sanxi was several months old and Martin in his twenty-fourth year, something happened to make the consent of the old landlord irrelevant. Martin "stole" a small quantity of grain from his father. Since they were both living in the same household, this theft probably reflected a struggle for power between the two heirs. But in any case theft was unpardonable by the Basque code, especially if done within the family. "The Basques are faithful," Judge Pierre de Lancre was to write; "they believe that theft is the work of a debased soul, of a low and abject heart; it bears witness to the demeaning neediness of a person." Martin Guerre had now placed himself in an imposssible situation. "For fear of the severity of his father," he left—he left his patrimony, his parents, his son, and his wife—and not one word was heard from him for many years.[9]

—————◆—————

It would be interesting to know whether Martin Guerre retraced his father's journey of two decades earlier and visited the Labourd. His status as heir was now in doubt, and he may not have wanted to see Johanto Daguerre and his other cousins lest they get word to his family of his whereabouts. But he would at least have viewed his birthplace and the waves off its shores. What is certain is that he crossed the Pyrenees into Spain, learned to speak Castilian, and ended up in Burgos as a lackey in the household of Francisco de Mendoza, a cardinal of the Roman Catholic Church.[10]

In 1550, Burgos was a flourishing city of some 19,000, still the commercial capital of Castille, center for the distribution of wool, and host to pilgrims going to Saint James of Compostela. Named bishop of its magnificent cathedral that year was Francisco de Mendoza y Bobadilla, former bishop of Coria, scholar and humanist, friend during their lifetimes of Erasmus and Vives, a cardinal since 1544, and part of the imperial party at the first session of the Council of Trent. Involved with high politics for the church and for Charles V, Don Francisco remained in Italy for several years. To present his letters of nomination to the cathedral chapter in August 1550, he sent his brother Pedro de Mendoza, a *comendador* of the Spanish military order of Santiago and captain in the Spanish army. Presumably Pedro saw to it as well that the household in the bishop's palace was running smoothly and could do business for the prelate during his absence.[11]

It was at this palace that the young peasant from Artigat must have become a lackey.* He was now at the bottom of a world of important men, of aristocratic canons from the cathedral, great merchants from the Ayuntamiento of Burgos, newly arrived Jesuits, and others who came and went in the bishop's household. He watched the elaborate ritual of the cathedral, a far cry from the parish mass at

---

*The phrase from Coras is: "this Martin Guerre, who went as a youth to Spain, where the Cardinal of Burgos and afterwards his brother made use of him as a lackey" (p. 137). Francisco de Mendoza did not reside in his bishopric until September 1557, and Martin had left Burgos at that time. I have assumed that he was a lackey at the bishop's palace in Burgos before Francisco's arrival. It is conceivable that somehow he became a servant in the cardinal's household in Rome and Siena—which would have introduced Martin Guerre to even more novelties—but there is no mention of an Italian stay by either Coras or Le Sueur. The Basques were prized as lackeys in the sixteenth century because of their alacrity. Gargantua has a Basque lackey; Montaigne speaks of their love of movement (Rabelais, *Gargantua*, ch. 28; Montaigne, *Essais*, III, ch. 13).

Bajou and Artigat. He moved about the crowded city with a sword and in the livery of one of the greatest houses of Spain. Did he ever have any regrets for the village he left behind or tell his confessor about his past?

Then Martin passed into the service of Francisco's brother Pedro, who had perhaps noticed his physical prowess, and as one of Pedro's entourage went into the Spanish army. At some point he was taken to Flanders and became part of the force that Philip II would use against the French at Saint-Quentin. It may never have occurred to him that he could be guilty of high treason. But then it may not have occurred to him that he would ever want to go back to France.

Wherever he was serving—either along with his master Pedro in the light cavalry or in the infantry—Martin survived the first days of the Spanish bombardment of the Picard town without injury. Then came August 10, Saint Lawrence's day, 1557, and the armies of Philip II routed the French troops who had come to relieve the besieged city, killing many men and taking prisoners, from the constable of France on down. "We collected much booty, weapons, horses, golden chains, silver and other things," a Spanish officer crowed in his journal. Pedro de Mendoza took two prisoners, for whom he received 300 écus in ransom. As for Martin Guerre, a French arquebus had hit him in the leg. It had to be amputated, and the days of Martin Guerre's agility were over.[12]

3

The Honor of Bertrande de Rols

····•————◆———•····

WHEN MARTIN GUERRE left on his adventures, his wife was no more than twenty-two years old. The "beautiful young woman" may also have looked at her past with some regrets.

As best we can see, Bertrande had spent her childhood with at least one brother and close to her mother's side, learning to spin and do other woman's work. Girls in Artigat and nearby villages were sometimes sent out to service in another household—we find a merchant's wife in Le Fossat leaving dresses to her servant, for example—but in families like Bertrande's they more often helped at home until they married.[1]

And then before Bertrande had time to dance to the violins with a village lad at the Assumption Day feast in Artigat or go through some other courtship ritual, she was wed to Martin Guerre. That she had started her "flowers," as the female menstrual flow was called, is probable, else the families would not have allowed the fertility drink the night of the wedding, intended to facilitate her pregnancy. But young as she was and in a strange house, she had the same sexual malaise as did Martin; she too was "bewitched," as she said to the court of Rieux years later. Now witches ordinarily dealt only with the male organ when trying to prevent intercourse between husband and wife.* But it could happen to a woman: as explained by the inquisitors in the *Malleus Maleficarum*, "the devil can so darken the wife's understanding that she considers her husband so loathsome that not for all the world would she allow him to lie with her."[2]

Bertrande might not have put it in these words, but it seems clear that for a while she was relieved that they could not have intercourse. Yet, when urged by her relatives to separate from Martin, she firmly refused. Here we come to certain character traits of Bertrande de Rols, which she was already displaying in her sixteenth year: a concern for her reputation as a woman, a stubborn independence, and a shrewd realism about how she could maneuver within the constraints placed upon one of her sex. Her refusal to have her marriage dissolved, which might well have been followed by another marriage at her parents' behest, freed her temporarily from certain wifely duties. It gave her a chance to have a girlhood with Martin's younger sisters, with whom she got on well. And she could get credit for her virtue. As Coras was to say of her refusal to separate from Martin, "that act, like a touchstone, offered great proof of the *honnesteté* of the said de Rols."[3] Some of the Artigat goodwives may have well uttered the same sentiments.

Then when Bertrande was ready for it, the old woman

---

*Indeed, while reporting Bertrande's words, Coras's annotation assumed that it was Martin who was under a spell and described only the forms of enchanting the male. Female "impotence" was due, he said, to natural causes, such as the woman's being "so narrow and closed in her secret parts that she could not endure carnal intercourse with a man" (pp.40–44). But this was not the case with Bertrande. The canonists also paid little attention to the occult causes of female impotence. Pierre Darmon, *Le Tribunal de l'impuissance* (Paris, 1979), pp. 48–52.

"appeared suddenly as if from heaven" and helped to lift the spell. She finally gave birth to a child, an event that meant for her (as it did for village women whose marriages began more smoothly) the first real step into adulthood. Bertrande had learned of that adult women's world from her own mother, from her Basque mother-in-law, and her godmothers. What did it hold in store for her? First, a world where organizational structure and public identity were associated exclusively with males. The particle "de," so often found in women's names in and around Artigat, did not come from the peasants trying to ape the nobility, but was a way of showing the classification system of village society. Ber-

Peasants dance, by Georges Reverdy, *Le Branle*, ca. 1555

trande was "de Rols," her father was Rols; Jeanne was "de Banquels," her father was Banquels; Arnaude was "de Tor," her father was Tor. The heirs along the Lèze River were always the male children, as we have seen, unless the family was unfortunate enough to have only girls. The village consuls summoned male villagers to their deliberations, convoking wives and widows only when there was an order to be given.[4]

In the everyday life of the fields and the households, however, the women were always important. They performed the characteristically female tasks of hoeing, trimming the vines, and cutting the grapes. Jointly with their husbands, they rented and worked the land, sheared sheep, and took cows and calves in contracts of *gasailhe*. A certain Maragille Cortalle, widow from Saint-Ybars, even acquired eighteen lambs by herself *en gasailhe*, promising to maintain them "as a good father of the family" for four years. They spun thread for the weavers of Le Fossat and made loaves of bread to sell to other villagers. Women like Marguerite alias La Brugarsse of Le Carla lent out small sums of money, while the wives and widows of rural merchants, such as Bertrande de Gouthelas and Suzanne de Robert of Le Fossat, made substantial sales in grain, millet, and wine. They were, of course, midwives, and with few surgeons resident in the area they did much of the curing.[5]

The women were most dependent on the good will of their husbands and sons when they were left as widows. In principle, the customs of the Languedoc guaranteed the widow the return of everything she had brought to the marriage as her dowry plus an "increase" of one third of the value of that dowry. In fact, in Artigat and surrounding burgs and villages, the marriage contracts do not say this. They spell out the wife's rights to the husband's estate only in the special case where her parents or widowed mother plan to live jointly with the couple. Most decisions are made in the husband's will. At best he provides that his wife can have the usufruct of all his goods so long as she lives "in widowhood" (some wills add "and in virtue"). If he really trusts her or wants to reward her "for her agreeable services," he specifies that she can enjoy his goods "without having to turn over accounts to anyone in the world." If she can not get along with his heirs, then he makes detailed provision for her: seven quarters of grain and one barrel of good wine each year, a dress and a pair of shoes and stockings every two years, wood for her heating, and the like. If she remarries, then he gives her a lump sum, which may be equivalent to her dowry or to her dowry and the increase.[6]

The realities of this peasant world encouraged not only the skills of a good farm wife, but the woman's ability to get her way with the men and to calculate her advantages, say, in remaining a widow. A wife of Artigat could never hope to have the position of the noble Rose d'Espaigne, Lady of Durfort, an heiress who was buying up lands and harassing her sharecroppers just to the east of the village. But she could hope to enjoy the respect of other village women and informal power as a widow, being addressed by the worthy title of Na, able to bestow a vineyard on a newly married son and hosen on all her godchildren. And the women seem to have gone along with the system, passing it on through the deep tie and hidden complicity of mother and daughter. As wives, they selected their husbands as their universal heirs; as widows, they usually preferred their sons as heirs over their daughters. They were deeply offended and sought redress when insulted as a "bagasse," a prostitute. Indeed, one goodwife of Le Fossat sued a neighbor woman, not only for hitting her in a quarrel over poultry but also for calling her a "hen."[7]

These were the values that Bertrande de Rols grew up with. In all her later adventures, Bertrande never showed herself as wanting to be outside this village society, to be rejected by it or to leave it. But she did seek to make her own way. It may have helped to have had the example close at hand of her mother-in-law, one of those self-assured Basque females. The women of the Labourd, often heirs and mistresses in their own right, were known for their "effrontery" and would later be notorious as witches.[8]

Just as Bertrande, now mother to a son, was establishing herself on a new footing with her mother-in-law, Martin Guerre disappeared without a trace. This was a catastrophe. Even for peasants who enjoyed a good gossip, the unexpected disappearance of an important villager was troubling, leaving an anomalous gap among the young married couples. For the Guerres from the Basque country, here was yet another scandal to live down. Martin's parents died without news of their son. The elder Sanxi finally forgave him, leaving a testament naming Martin as heir both to the property in Hendaye and the lands in Artigat. The local notaries knew what to do when the universal heir was absent: "if he is dead or does not return," the formulas went, others are substituted in his place. For the time being, Pierre Guerre would be the administrator of the considerable properties of his late brother and the guardian of Martin's unmarried sisters.[9]

At some point in those years—most likely in the early 1550's in the wake of the elder Sanxi's death—Pierre Guerre made an effort to salvage the relationship between the Guerres and the Rols and to help Martin's abandoned wife. Now a widower with daughters of his own, he married Bertrande's widowed mother.* Their marriage contract would have been of the elaborate kind, drawn up at the establishment of a joint household. Bertrande's mother would have brought whatever money or goods her husband had left her in the event that she remarried; Pierre would have made promises to support Bertrande and her son Sanxi; and they would have decided how to share any newly acquired goods. The neighboring house in which the old landlord and the young landlord had lived was presumably leased for short terms—no one would have trusted the young Bertrande to maintain it under the circumstances—and Pierre Guerre took over the headship of a household of mostly females on his own land.

Bertrande's status was much reduced by all these events. Neither wife nor widow, she was under the same roof with her mother again. Neither wife nor widow, she had to face the other village women at the mill, the well, the tileworks, and at the harvest. And there was no easy remedy for her in the law. Since the laxer days of Pope Alexander III in the twelfth century, the doctors had insisted that a wife was not free to remarry in the absence of her husband, no matter how many years had elapsed, unless she had certain proof of his death. Of the alternate traditions in the civil law, it was the harsher one of Justinian that had prevailed. The Parlement of Toulouse cited it in judging a marriage case in 1557: "During the absence of the husband, the wife cannot remarry unless she has proof of his death . . . not even when he has been absent twenty years or more . . . And the death

---

*Coras does not give the date of the marriage of Pierre Guerre and Bertrande's mother (pp. 67–68), but this seems the most probable time. Pierre's daughters are never referred to as sisters or half-sisters of Bertrande, and he must have had them by a first marriage. Whatever economic arrangements her husband had made for her in his will, Bertrande's mother would have been induced by her daughter's predicament to remarry.

must be proven by witnesses, who give sure depositions, or by great and manifest presumptions."[10]

Of course peasants might try to get around the law—it would hardly be the first time—and fabricate news of a drowning or a bullet, or simply ignore the law if there were a cooperative priest in the village. But Bertrande chose not to do so. Her practical interest kept her close to her son and what would some day be his inheritance. There was also her stiff-necked sense of herself and her reputation. Whatever glances or invitations came her way, the beautiful young woman lived (so everyone would later attest) "virtuously and honorably."[11]

Meanwhile she worked, she raised her son Sanxi, and she waited. She may have been helped through her solitude by her four sisters-in-law and by the wise woman who had counseled her during her bewitchment. The rectors who had succeeded Messire Jacques Boëri in the church of Artigat were neither of them from local families and may not have always resided in the parish; Bertrande may have elaborated on her troubles only to Saint Catherine, whose chapel was in the cemetery.[12] But she surely reflected on her life, dividing it into thirds as she did later when presenting herself to the judge of Rieux: the nine or ten years of her childhood, the nine or ten years of her marriage, the years of her waiting, which lengthened into eight or more.[13] Beyond a young womanhood with only a brief period of sexuality, beyond a marriage in which her husband understood her little, may have feared her, and surely abandoned her, Bertrande dreamed of a husband and lover who would come back, and be different. Then in the summer of 1556, a man presented himself to her as the long-lost Martin Guerre. Previously he had been known as Arnaud du Tilh, alias Pansette.

4

The Masks of Arnaud du Tilh

····•————◄━◆━►————•····

D U TILH WAS A commonplace name in Gascony and
Languedoc, and often heard in the diocese of Lombez,
where Arnaud was born. His father Arnaud Guilhem du
Tilh had his roots there in the village of Sajas; his mother, a
Barrau, came from nearby Le Pin. These places were to the
northwest of the diocese of Rieux and well beyond the
Garonne; it would take a good day's ride to get from Sajas
to Artigat.

Contemporaries called Arnaud's country the Comminges.
"Rich in grains," his compatriot François de Belleforest
wrote about it, "rich in wines, fruits, hay, walnut oil, millet,
and other things necessary for life. The Comminges
abounds in men, as brave fighters as could be . . . and there
are innumerable large burgs, rich villages, and ancient cas-
tles, with more nobles than in any other part of France."[1]

Arnaud du Tilh would probably have described his country in less glowing terms. Sajas had its seignior, Jean de Vize
and then his son Séverie; the powerful old house of Com-
minges-Péguilhan possessed the seigniory of Le Pin. This
could mean not only the usual payments but also interfer-
ence in village life, as in Mane where the seignior tried to
limit the inhabitants' rights to have a tavern and a butcher-

shop. The "abundance of people" could mean not only extra arms for farm work but also pressure on the supply of land; the notaries in the diocese of Lombez often found themselves drawing up contracts for sharecropping.[2]

It was an active economic region, however, caught up in the orbit of Toulouse. Peasants from Sajas and Le Pin went to Rieumes and farther away to L'Isle-en-Dodon, Lombez, Gimont, and Toulouse to buy or sell grain, wine, cloth, and wood; to take on sheep, goats, and oxen *en gasailhe*; and to deliver fleece and skins. Sajas itself was one of the smaller villages in the vicinity of Rieumes. On its hills and slopes lived some thirty to forty families, most of them in farming and herding, several involved in weaving linen cloth and in a few other rural crafts. Le Pin was larger, more the size of Artigat and with a wider range of artisans, though the first resident notary probably appeared only in the seventeenth century.[3]

The du Tilhs and the Barraus were quite ordinary families in this rural society. In 1551, when a diocesan visitation came round, they are not listed among the consuls and *bassiniers* of their villages—not among the Dabeyats, Daubans, de Soles, and Saint Andrieus who deliberated on local matters and took charge of the parish vestry. Instead they stood among the middle ranks of the peasants, with enough fields and vineyards so that when Arnaud Guilhem died and divided his property equally among his sons (the practice in Sajas and Le Pin as it was in Artigat), there would be a little land for Arnaud.[4]

The one thing noteworthy about the du Tilhs was their son Arnaud. His youth was the opposite of Martin Guerre's. He grew up in a family of boys, with whom he got on well. He was rather short and stocky, and not especially adept at the village sports. But he was wonderfully fluent of tongue and had a memory an actor would envy. He was the kind of lad whom the vicars of Sajas, almost the only people in the village who could sign their names, would have identified as a potential priest and sent off to school.[5]

If they tried, they must have been sorely disappointed. Arnaud du Tilh became known as "dissolute," a youth of "bad life," "absorbed in every vice." This meant drinking and sexual adventures, perhaps at the taverns of Rieumes, perhaps with the prostitutes at Toulouse. He became known as Pansette, "the belly," a man with big appetites, and he must have loved the carnivals, the costuming, the dancing, and all the games of the festive "youth abbeys" (youth groups), which were so marked a part of village life in Gascony. He was quicktempered and heard to swear often on the head, body, blood, and wounds of Christ, not as offensive perhaps as insulting the Virgin Mary but nonetheless associated with riotous people, who played cards and gambled. So clever was Pansette that he began to be suspected of magic, almost a compliment when one realizes that it was said not about an old crone but about a gregarious youth in his early twenties.[6]

In his way, Arnaud du Tilh was as much at odds with family and peasant property as was Martin Guerre in Artigat. Though his doings took him down to Pouy-de-Touges and as far away as Toulouse, he restlessly dreamed of something beyond the seigniory of Sajas, beyond the hills of the Diocese of Lombez. There was always the possibility of the king's band of foot soldiers, those "adventurers" among whom the Gascons loomed so large. The notaries at Gimont were often called upon to draw up wills for the soldiers going off to war from the region. After a series of petty thefts, Pansette left to serve Henri II on the battlefields of Picardy.[7]

Did the two runaways ever meet before Arnaud du Tilh decided to impersonate Martin Guerre? In her complaint to the judge of Rieux, Bertrande de Rols said that they might have known each other as fellow soldiers—"and the said du Tilh, as is plausible, could have accompanied the said Martin to war and, under pretext of friendship, heard from him numerous private and particular things about himself and his wife"—a suggestion that led Coras to write an annotation on friendship and its betrayal. One line of Arnaud's testimony at Rieux could support some prior connection between the two, that is, his report of the places and people that Martin Guerre had allegedly visited in France and Spain during his absence, all of which was subsequently verified by the court. This information could have come from Martin, or from others that knew him. But it is hard to see how they could have been intimates in the army, since Martin was fighting for the king of Spain, the enemy of the king of France, and Arnaud may have returned from Picardy before Martin had even left Burgos.[8]

Still, the two young men may have met in their wanderings around the region or elsewhere. As a "thought experiment," let us imagine what might have taken place if the heir from Artigat became friends with the golden-tongued peasant from Sajas. They learn that they look alike, even though Martin is taller, thinner, and a little darker than Arnaud. They hear this from other people rather than observing it, for sixteenth-century villagers do not build up an image of their faces by frequent glances in a mirror (an object not found in a peasant household). It is unsettling and fascinating, and since there is a stock of popular sayings about how the shape of the eye or the set of the jaw signify certain character traits,[9] they wonder whether their resemblance is more than skin-deep. They exchange confidences. Martin expresses himself with ambivalence about his patrimony and his wife, perhaps seems to imply to his look-alike, "take her." And Pansette says to himself, "Why not?" At any rate, one of the few things Arnaud later confided to a Sajas acquaintance during his Artigat days was, "Martin Guerre is dead, he gave me his goods."[10]

This is a possible scenario, but it is not the one to which Arnaud du Tilh finally confessed. He claimed he had never encountered Martin Guerre before he went to Artigat. If true, this makes the imposture all the more interesting (more marvelous, "mirabilis magis", said the pamphleteer Le Sucur) and more psychologically probable: it represents the difference between making another person's life your own and merely imitating him. Arnaud had come back from the army camp in Picardy around 1553, presumably after the battles of Thérouanne, Hesdin, and Valenciennes. Passing through Mane along the Salat River one day, he encountered two friends of Martin, Master Dominique Pujol and the hotelkeeper Pierre de Guilhet, who took him for the missing man from Artigat.[11]

At this point the trickster in Pansette snapped to attention. He informed himself as cunningly as he could about Martin Guerre, his situation, his family, and the things he used to say and do. He worked through Pujol, Guilhet, and "other familiar friends and neighbors" of the Guerres, and the first two may actually have become his accomplices.[12] In that world of busy motion, he could get information through the gossip networks without actually going to Artigat—and it was plentiful, including domestic details, such as the location of the white hosen that Martin had left in a certain trunk before he had departed. He learned the names of many of the villagers and about Martin's relations with them. He inquired about the Labourd and picked up a few words of Basque. It took many months for Arnaud to prepare his role, for he arrived in Artigat only in 1556. (It is unknown where Arnaud was living during this period of preparation. He may not have gone back to Sajas and his old "life of dissolution.")

Was it so unusual for a man in sixteenth-century villages and burgs to change his name and fashion a new identity? Some of this went on all the time. The Daguerres left Hendaye, became the Guerres, and changed their ways. Every peasant who migrated any distance might be expected to do the same. And whether you moved or not, you might acquire a nickname, an alias. In Artigat it often had to do with your property, and in Sajas it had to do with you: one of Arnaud's fellow villagers was nicknamed Tambourin,[13] the drum, and he of course was Pansette.

But to take on a false identity? At carnival time and at other feastdays, a young peasant might dress as an animal or as a person of another estate or sex and speak through that disguise. In a charivari, one villager might play another, might serve as a stand-in for the person being humiliated for his or her inappropriate marriage or bad marital conduct. But these were temporary masks and intended for the common good.

There was also more self-interested deception: healthy beggars pretending to be lame or blind and people counterfeiting an identity to collect an inheritance or otherwise gain some economic advantage. Storytellers recounted the History of the Three Brothers: two impostors who tried to claim the inheritance of the true son; the prince found out who the latter was by ordering the three of them to shoot arrows at the father's corpse. Real people tried it too. In

1557, for instance, a certain Aurelio Chitracha, native of Damascus, arrived in Lyon, assumed the name of the late Vallier Trony, and went about collecting sums due to Trony until the nuns to whom Trony's goods had been adjudged discovered the hoax and had him arrested. The same year, only a few streets away, Antoine Ferlaz and Jean Fontanel were busily claiming to be Michel Mure; each chose a different notary and was issuing IOU's and receipts in his name until Mure found out about it.[14]

Now Arnaud du Tilh surely had something to gain in his move from Sajas to Artigat, for Martin Guerre's inheritance was larger than his own. But it is clear that in his elaborate preparations, his investigations, his memorization—even perhaps his rehearsals—Pansette was moving beyond the mask of the carnival player and the strategems of the mere inheritance seeker to forge a new identity and a new life for himself in the village on the Lèze.

5
The Invented Marriage

⋯•⸺◈⸺•⋯

THE NEW MARTIN did not go straight to Artigat. As Le
Sueur reported it, he went first to a hostelry at the next
village, probably Pailhès. He told the hotelkeeper he was
Martin Guerre and wept when his wife and family were
mentioned. The word spread to his four sisters, who rushed
to the inn, greeted him with delight, and went back for
Bertrande. When she saw him, however, she recoiled in
surprise. Not until he had spoken to her affectionately, re-
minding her of things they had done and talked about, specifically mentioning the white hosen in the trunk, did she
fall upon his neck and kiss him; it was his beard that had
made him hard to recognize. Pierre Guerre looked him over
steadily as well and did not believe he was his nephew until
he reminisced about their activities together. Finally Pierre
embraced him and thanked God for his return.

Even then the new Martin did not leave for Artigat, but
stayed at the hostelry to rest from his trip and recover from
an illness. (Le Sueur claims he had the pox and was showing a curious fineness of conscience in protecting Bertrande's body from syphilis when he was about to defile her
soul and her marriage bed.) This gave Bertrande the chance
to take care of him and gradually get used to him. This gave

him the chance to learn more about the past of Martin Guerre. When he was better, she took him back to his house, welcomed him as her husband, and helped him get reacquainted with the villagers.

The new Martin's reception in Artigat had much the same character. He greeted people by name and, if they seemed not to recognize him, talked to them about the things they had done together ten or fifteen years before. He explained to everyone that he had been off serving in the army of the king of France, had spent some months in Spain, and was now eager to be once again in his village with his relatives, his son Sanxi, and especially his wife Bertrande.[1]

I think we can account for the initial acceptance by family and neighbors without having recourse to the necromancy of which Arnaud was later accused and which he always denied. First of all, he was wanted in Artigat—wanted with ambivalence perhaps, for returning persons always dash some hopes and disturb power relations, but wanted more than not. The heir and householder Martin Guerre was back in his place. Second, he came announced, predisposing people to perceive him as Martin Guerre.[2] Then this perception was confirmed by his compelling words and his accurate memories. It was true that he did not look exactly the same as the Martin Guerre who had left. But then the Guerres had no painted portraits by which to recall his features, and it might be thought natural for a man to fill out as he grew older and for a peasant to be changed by years of soldiering. Thus whatever doubts people had, they silenced or even buried them for a while and allowed the new Martin to grow into his role.

What of Bertrande de Rols? Did she know that the new

Martin was not the man who had abandoned her eight years before? Perhaps not at the very first, when he arrived with all his "signs" and proofs. But the obstinate and honorable Bertrande does not seem a woman so easily fooled, not even by a charmer like Pansette. By the time she had received him in her bed, she must have realized the difference; as any wife of Artigat would have agreed, there is no mistaking "the touch of the man on the woman."[3] Either by explicit or tacit agreement, she helped him become her husband. What Bertrande had with the new Martin was her dream come true, a man she could live with in peace and friendship (to cite sixteenth-century values) and in passion.

It was an invented marriage, not arranged like her own of eighteen years earlier or contracted in a customary way like that of her mother and Pierre Guerre. It started off with a lie but, as Bertrande described it later, they passed their time "like true married people, eating, drinking, and sleeping together." According to Le Sueur, the "Pseudo-Martinus" lived with Bertrande "quietly, without strife, and conducted himself so well in every way with her that no one could suspect any deceit." In the marriage bed of the beautiful Bertrande things now went well. Within three years, two daughters were born to them; one died, but the other, Bernarde, became Sanxi's little sister.[4]

The evidence for the relationship between the new Martin and Bertrande comes not from this peaceful period of three years, but from the time when the invented marriage was called into doubt. Yet it everywhere attests to his having fallen in love with the wife for whom he had rehearsed and her having become deeply attached to the husband who had taken her by surprise. When he is released from prison in the midst of later quarrels, she gives him a white shirt, washes his feet, and receives him back into her bed. When

A rural couple from Roussillon, south of Artigat, 1529, from
Das Tractenbuch des Christoph Weiditz

others try to kill him, she puts her body between him and the blows. Before the court he addresses her "gently"; he puts his life in her hands by saying that if she swears that he is not her husband he will submit "to a thousand cruel deaths."[5]

In happier times, they talked together. It was "in conversing day and night" that the new Martin added to his store of information about Bertrande, the Guerres, and Artigat. Such intimate exchanges between husband and wife in the sixteenth century are thought to be an ideal of Christian humanists and Protestant moralists, realized, if at all, in households much more elevated than those of Artigat. But as Le Roy Ladurie has suggested for an earlier period, the Occitan delight in conversation was expressed not only at the evening gathering among neighbors, but also in the words of peasant lovers.[6] The new Martin certainly had more to discuss with Bertrande than the crops, the sheep, and the children. Among other things, so one must surmise, they decided to make the invented marriage last.

Such an action may have been easier to justify for people coming out of centuries of peasant experience in manipulating popular rituals and the Catholic law on marriage. From the late twelfth century to 1564, what made a marriage in canon law was the consent of the partners and their consent alone; if they took each other as husband and wife in words of the present, even in the absence of the priest or any witness, exchanged tokens of consent, and especially if they then went on to have intercourse, they were joined in an indissoluble union. The church disapproved of this "clandestine" path to marriage,* but there were always

---

*As Beatrice Gottlieb writes, "casuists and lawyers discussed clandestine marriage as a sin and a nuisance" ("The Meaning of Clandestine Marriage," in R. Wheaton and T. K. Haraven, eds., *Family and Sexuality in French History*

some people, especially in the villages, who used it for reasons of their own: they were minors and their parents were opposed to the marriage; they were marrying within a prohibited degree of kinship and could not get a dispensation; they wanted to have intercourse and this was the only way to do it; one of the partners was already married to a person in another place.[7]

What this tradition offered to the couple in Artigat was no quick solution to their particular predicament. The new Martin was dealing after all with a clandestine identity, and Bertrande would have had difficulty in squaring possible bigamy with her sense of honor, not to mention her conscience. But it did allow them the possibility of *conceiving* of marriage as something that was in their hands to make, indeed, as in their hands alone.

What was not, by any stretch of the imagination, under their control by Catholic teaching was their souls. Though eventually both of them were to express guilt about their behavior, it is unlikely that they ever confessed their sins fully to the priests of Artigat or Bajou. From all accounts they were considered to be a respectable couple during the years of peaceable marriage; any priest who had heard at Easter confession that the new Martin had once been Pansette would have excommunicated them as notorious adulterers unless they separated immediately. This raises the

[Philadelphia, 1980], p.52). It was a nuisance because of the many cases of breach of promise or bigamy which came up before the spiritual courts, and one could hardly establish proof when there were no witnesses. At the last session of the Council of Trent in 1564, the Church determined that for a marriage to be valid it must henceforth be preceded by the reading of banns and performed by a parish priest. It took a long time for the clergy to put a stop to the older practice. In France the main complaint was that clandestine marriage allowed children to make a valid and indissoluble union without the consent of their parents. In February 1557, Henri II issued an edict on clandestine marriages, which was to be the subject of a treatise by Jean de Coras.

whole question of Protestantism in Artigat. It is possible, even probable, that the new Martin and Bertrande de Rols were becoming interested in the new religion, in part because they could draw from it another justification for their lives.

Protestant proselytizers were spreading the word in the county of Foix by 1536, and people were already leaving Pamiers and Le Mas-d'Azil for Geneva in 1551. After 1557 the movement grew in strength, and in 1561 Le Mas, encouraged by the example of its Protestant countess Jeanne d'Albret, pronounced itself a Reformed town. Le Carla, even closer to Artigat, became a bastion of the Reformed Church. There were stirrings also in the villages and burgs along the Lèze River. The conservative Catholic Jacques de Villemur, seignior of Pailhès, kept a tight hand on his peasants, but in Le Fossat there was an important group of families "suspected of the new religion" in 1563. In 1568 the church of Artigat was cleansed of its "idols" and its altar smashed, not merely by Reformed soldiers but also by local converts. A later diocesan visitation referred to this as a period when "the inhabitants of the said Artigat were Huguenots."[8]

A movement of this amplitude must be prepared for. It means that a decade earlier in the traffic that linked Artigat with Pamiers, Le Fossat, Saint-Ybars, Le Carla, and Le Mas-d'Azil, Protestant ideas were flowing along with the fleece, grain, and wine. It means that Antoine Caffer, the pastor from Geneva who was preaching in the Saint-Vincent cemetery at Foix in 1556, passed through Artigat as well. It means that someone in the village had a Reformed New Testament or a Protestant tract in French and was reading it aloud in langue d'oc to his neighbors. Even if they were still having their infants baptized at the Catholic fonts, some of the people listening to the priest were looking forward to the day when a Protestant pastor would take the curate's place. Meanwhile the local clergy were not in the best position to fight back. When Messire Pierre Laurens du Caylar became rector of Artigat around 1553, he had to face a court case with a competing candidate, resolved only by the Parlement of Toulouse. (The same thing had happened to Dominique de Claveria in the 1540s and to Jacques Boëri in the 1530s.) The parish priest of Bajou was one of the Drot brothers, from a modest family and unable to carry much weight in the village.[9]

What evidence is there that our invented couple was touched by the new teaching? First, the Rols family became Protestant: they bestowed Old Testament names like Abraham on their children, and in the seventeenth century, when most Artigatois were good Catholics, there were still Rolses trudging over to Le Carla for Reformed services.[10] As for the new Martin, I doubt that he arrived in Artigat already convinced of the Gospel of the Word. The bishop of Lombez, Antoine Olivier, was thought to be a Protestant sympathizer and there was an important Protestant movement in Arnaud's diocese,[11] but the ex-soldier Arnaud du Tilh had other things on his mind between 1553 and 1556 and may not have been residing in Sajas. Instead I think he became open to the new ideas in Artigat, where the life he was fashioning for himself was operating like a conversion experience, wiping away the blasphemer, the young man "of bad life," if not totally the trickster.

Whatever the case, it is significant that no priest of Artigat or Bajou played a major role in the subsequent trials of the new Martin at Rieux and Toulouse. They must have been among the one hundred and eighty witnesses heard before the case was through, but what they had to say did not find its way into Coras's summary of all the telling evidence on either side. Also significant is the respect that the new Martin showed for the two judges delegated to question him, Jean de Coras and François de Ferrières, men who were already attracted to Protestantism in 1560 and who became its staunchest supporters in the Parlement of Toulouse. He asked that they return for his final confession, which included no Catholic formulas or references to the saints, but sought only God's mercy for sinners who placed their hope in Christ on the cross.[12]

What hope might the Protestant message have offered to the new Martin and Bertrande during the years they were living together as "true married people"? That they could tell their story to God alone and need not communicate it to any human intermediary. That the life they had willfully fabricated was part of God's providence. Perhaps too they heard some echoes of the new marriage law established in Reformed Geneva after 1545. There, marriage was no longer a sacrament; and a wife abandoned by her husband, "without the wife having given him any occasion or being in any way guilty," could after a year of inquiry obtain from the Consistory a divorce and permission to remarry.[13]

But even if they did appropriate and apply such ideas to themselves, they must have realized that there was still no sure way ahead. How to explain to a Reformed Consistory the rebirth of Arnaud du Tilh as Martin Guerre? The new Martin had won over Bertrande de Rols as his accomplice, at least for a time, but could an impostor count on the other people in Artigat?

6

Quarrels

....•———◀◆▶———•....

THE NEW MARTIN was not only a husband, but also an heir, a nephew, and an important peasant proprietor in Artigat. It was in these roles that the trouble finally began.

The house that had once belonged to the elder Sanxi Guerre now became the home of the new Martin. His two unmarried sisters probably moved back in with him, as would be expected in Basque custom. From there, he and Bertrande took part in the village world of hospitality, god-parentage, and exchange, visiting with Pierre Guerre and his wife (Bertrande's mother, we remember), Martin Guerre's married sisters, Bertrande's brother, and other neighbors and friends who were to testify about his identity later on. Catherine Boëri, who years before had brought the ineffective potion to Bertrande's marriage bed, the Lozes from Pailhès, the Del Pech family, saddlers from Le Carla, James Delhure and his wife Bernarde Arzel of Pamiers and Artigat (Bernarde was perhaps the godmother of the baby Bernarde Guerre) were all part of their circle of comfortable rural families.[1]

Nor was the step into farm life hard for the new Martin; wheat, millet, vines, and sheep were what he already knew from the diocese of Lombez. There were also tileworks in the vicinity of Sajas, but since bricks are not listed among the transactions of the new Martin, it seems that Pierre Guerre maintained control over this family enterprise. What was impressive was how the new Martin developed the Guerre holdings in a commercial direction; he became a rural "merchant" like Jean Banquels, dealing in grains, wine, and wool up and down the Lèze and farther. In Artigat it would be difficult to become the lessor-manager of a great estate—the most successful path for a rural capitalist in Languedoc—for there were no noble or abbatial properties within the jurisdiction. Perhaps he was able to join the men who rented the benefice of Artigat in 1558 and 1559 (there is a lacuna in the accounts for those years), but he certainly became involved in buying, selling, and leasing land. That is to say, he tried to take commercial advantage of the properties that Sanxi Guerre had carefully acquired in Artigat and passed on to his heir Martin.[2]

Bertrande de Rols must have been delighted with this turn of events, for the wife of a rural merchant often became a merchant herself. But Pierre Guerre began to balk. At first he had been glad to have his nephew in the village and had bragged about him to his cronies, such as Jean Loze, a consul of Pailhès. Then the new Martin started to sell parcels of the *propres*, a practice not uncommon in the active land market of the Lèze valley, as we have seen, but not in accord with Basque custom. When he proposed to put a new lease on some ancestral property in Hendaye, or even to sell it, Pierre Guerre must have been horrified.[3]

Meanwhile Martin embarked on another course of action that brought the powerful Guerre anger to the fore. He asked Pierre to give him the accounts he had kept after the elder Sanxi's death, when he had been administrator of his nephew's property. He asked him nicely—"in fair words," which the gifted Pansette always had on the tip of his tongue—but suspected that Pierre was withholding some of the inheritance, and in any case he wanted the profits Pierre had collected from it. For a long time they bantered about this good-naturedly, but finally in late 1558 or early 1559 the new Martin brought a civil suit against Pierre before the judge of Rieux.*

Such actions were not unheard of among peasant families. By the customs of the Labourd, Pierre would have been expected to have an inventory made of his nephew's goods at the start of his administration and to put down a deposit as guarantee that he would return them in good condition. In the diocese of Rieux, widows with rights to their husband's goods were expected to turn accounts over to their children when they came of age unless the husband had specifically provided that they "were not to be bothered." Indeed, in Artigat the amicable handing over of a guardian's accounts and the revenues from the property was done before a notary, just so there would be no misunderstanding.[4]

For Pierre Guerre, however, the new Martin had gone too far. It may be that he felt the circumstances of Martin's absence did not entitle him to any rewards. It may be that he felt a nephew whom he had "brought up from childhood" should not require such contractual arrangements and certainly should not resort to litigation. It may be that the old patriarch resented the challenge to his authority; he had said no and he meant no. Perhaps it was simply what the new

---

*All that Coras reports on this suit is that the new Martin "was constrained to prosecute [Pierre Guerre] before the court for the recovery of his goods: but as for the profits and the turning over of accounts, the uncle Pierre Guerre would hear nothing of it" (pp. 33–34). This sounds like a settlement in which Pierre agreed to turn over the rest of the inheritance and the new Martin agreed to drop the demand for the accounts and for what was left of the revenues.

Martin claimed it was—"avarice," the desire to keep the goods and revenues for his own household, his daughters and sons-in-law.

At any rate, the doubts that the nimble Martin had quieted at his first appearance now came into the open and proliferated in Pierre's mind. Why had he forgotten so many Basque phrases, some of which must have been bandied about all throughout his childhood? Why was he no longer interested in swordplay and acrobatics? That stocky body he had accepted as his nephew's adult form now seemed alien. When he looked carefully at Sanxi, the boy did not resemble the man sharing Bertrande's bed. Above all, "the Basque is faithful." For a small theft of grain from his father, Martin Guerre had left his patrimony in dishonor. Now an impostor was in the process of shamelessly stealing it from the heir.[5]

Pierre convinced his wife and sons-in-law of the terrible truth. Bertrande's mother was in complete accord with her husband, not only as an obedient spouse but also as a practical woman and a good mother, devoted to the best interests of her daughter. Hadn't she begged Bertrande years before to separate from Martin and make a better match during his years of impotence? Now she must save her daughter from the dishonor of adultery. Together they pressed Bertrande to bring a case against the man she was living with. Bertrande stubbornly refused.

For the next year and more the Guerre family was divided, and the quarrel spread to the whole village and beyond. Pierre Guerre went about telling everyone that the new Martin was a faker who had tricked him. He asked his friend Jean Loze to help him put up money to have the impostor killed. Loze refused, shocked that he would harm his nephew. Martin went about saying that his uncle had made up this story because he had asked for the accounts. The village shoemaker said that, if he were Martin Guerre, why had his feet grown so much smaller over the years? Martin's sisters insisted that the new Martin was their brother (they may have preferred him to their uncle as head of the family and its property); Pierre's sons-in-law insisted that the new Martin was a liar. (What Bertrande's brother said is not reported.) Bertrande was ferocious in defense of him as "Martin Guerre her husband": "He is Martin Guerre my husband [she is reported as saying] or else some devil in his skin. I know him well. If anyone is so mad as to say the contrary, I'll make him die." And then when Pierre Guerre and his sons-in-law beat him with a club, Bertrande protected him, as has been recounted, by her own body.[6]

The consuls of Artigat undoubtedly discussed the matter of Martin Guerre at many meetings in the spring and summer of 1559. With opinion so split in the village, they could never have arbitrated the dispute. For some, the new Martin was an upstanding householder, husband, and rural merchant, unjustly slandered by a greedy uncle; for others, he was a glib impostor robbing an established family of its reputation. Still others were unsure where the truth lay. On both sides the rural family is prized, but on the one more weight is given to the wishes of the younger generation to go off and see the world for a while, and to make decisions for itself about how property is to be used; and on the other more weight is given to the decisions of the elders and to long-term continuity in family behavior.

It would be interesting to know if this difference of opinion converged with any other differences that cut across village society. Coras tells us that there were about as many supporters of the new Martin as there were of Pierre Guerre in and around Artigat, but outside the Guerre family he reports specific positions in only three instances: Catherine Boëri and Jean Loze supported Martin and the shoemaker supported Pierre. What is sure is that Artigat was not structured along strict clan lines, such as those that divided Montaillou between the Clergues and the Azémas some two hundred and fifty years before. Rather it had political institutions that favored alliances among the top families in Artigat and neighboring villages. The Banquels, the Lozes, and the Boëris had their own circles and dependents, but we can see from notarial contracts that they overlapped. Quarrels that broke out, like this one, did not always follow strict lines of family.[7] If I were to hazard a guess about the Martin Guerre case, it would be that the local Protestant sympathizers tended to believe the new Martin and the Catholics tended to believe Pierre Guerre.

Be that as it may, in the late summer and fall of 1559, two events occured that made the situation of Martin and Bertrande much worse. A soldier from Rochefort passed through Artigat and, seeing the disputed man, announced to witnesses that he was a deceiver. Martin Guerre had been in Flanders and had lost a leg two years before during the siege of Saint-Quentin. The real Martin Guerre had a wooden leg, the soldier said, and then went on his way.[8]

So after eleven years the original Martin Guerre was perhaps still alive, and the proofs of the new Martin's fabrication were multiplying. It seemed more and more likely that Pierre Guerre would find a way to take the impostor to court. The couple had to be prepared to counter his arguments, and now they probably worked out the strategy they would eventually follow during the trials. His testimony must be as complete as posssible on every aspect of the life of Martin Guerre, from the Labourd on, and must always match her testimony; there must be intimate details that no one could challenge. Maybe then the court would rule that he was the real Martin Guerre and Bertrande's stepfather would be silenced.

So Pansette's rehearsals began once again. The old life was gone over yet another time, the wedding, the festivities, the impotence relived, the breaking of the spell reexperienced. Bertrande searched her memory for a sexual episode—perhaps even embroidered it—with which they could surprise the court. (Coras said later of such testimony that it was "very much easier to understand than it was to tell or write down.")[9]

Then came another blow. A farm building belonging to Jean d'Escornebeuf, seignior of Lanoux, was burned down, and he accused the new Martin of arson and had the sénéchal of Toulouse imprison him in that city. The Escornebeufs were part of the petty nobility in the Lèze valley, with Jean's properties located in the parish just to the west of Artigat. He had been buying land in Artigat, however, and in 1550 was one of those taking on the lease of its benefice along with Antoine Banquels and others. Perhaps his building had in fact been set ablaze by some farmers of Artigat who resented the penetration of a gentleman into a village so proud that it had no seignior. But it was the upstart peasant-merchant Martin Guerre, the center of scandal, whom Escornebeuf took as his target, and in the course of his complaint—evidently tipped off by Pierre Guerre—he told the judge that the prisoner "had usurped the marriage bed of another man."[10]

Bertrande was in great distress. She seems to have moved her household back in once more with her mother and Pierre Guerre.[11] She went to Toulouse (perhaps her first trip there in all her thirty-two years), brought money and other necessities to Martin in prison, and made known her view that this man was her husband and that Pierre Guerre and his wife were trying to coerce her to accuse him falsely. Escornebeuf's evidence against the new Martin was not very good. Had he been the seignior of Artigat, he might have prevailed, but before the Sénéchaussée of Toulouse he had to drop the arson charge and the prisoner was released.[12]

In the meantime Pierre Guerre had taken steps to find out who the deceiver really was. In this region of comings and goings and of extensive gossip, it is surprising that he had not discovered anything earlier. The new Martin himself had left clues in the course of his travels. At Pouy-de-Touges, for example, a village south of Sajas falling within the diocese of Rieux, he had been recognized as Arnaud du Tilh by the innkeeper; he had asked him to say nothing, for "Martin Guerre is dead; he has given me his goods." A certain Pelegrin de Liberos had called him Pansette; the new Martin had hushed him but fell out of character sufficiently to give him two handkerchiefs to take to his brother, Jean du Tilh.[13]

Some such story got back to Pierre Guerre, and now he could give another name to the traitor in their midst: Arnaud du Tilh alias Pansette, a man of bad life from Sajas. To catch the liar, though, he would have to lie. He falsely presented himself to the judge of Rieux as agent for Bertrande de Rols. (Possibly he did it with a notarized document; when Master Jean Pegulha came from Le Fossat to Artigat to draw up contracts, he often used Pierre Guerre's house as a place to work.) In Bertrande's name he got permission to have a formal inquiry opened about the man calling himself Martin Guerre and to have him immediately made prisoner with the use of several armed men, as the law allowed in those special cases where the accused was thought likely to flee and "to have a very bad reputation, reviled for several enormous offenses."[14]

When the new Martin returned from prison in Toulouse in January 1560, Pierre was ready for him. Bertrande received him with tenderness, washing his feet and taking him into her bed. Very early the next morning, Pierre and his sons-in-law, all armed, seized him in Bertrande's name and had him bundled off to prison in Rieux.[15]

Let us pause here a moment and ask whether such a situation was inevitable. To put it another way, if the real Martin Guerre had never come back, could Arnaud du Tilh have gotten away with it? Some of my pragmatic fellow historians have suggested that, if the impostor had not asked for the accounts and had followed more closely the uncle's expectations in regard to the family property, he could have played Martin Guerre for years and no one would have minded. On the other hand, recently when I talked about Bertrande and Arnaud with people in Artigat who were still familiar with the old story, they smiled, shrugged their shoulders, and said, "That's all very well—but that pretty rascal, he lied."

I think the people in Artigat are closer to the mark. Not that Arnaud du Tilh, with more prudence and foresight, might not have arranged a different scenario for himself. Not that Arnaud was the only liar in Artigat: we have just caught Pierre Guerre in a falsehood, and we will hear of others before we are done. But a big lie, a whopper—especially one imposed by a single person on others—has troublesome consequences both for personal feelings and for social relationships.[16]

From the villagers and from the Guerre family, who to some extent had to give assent to his lie, Arnaud required constant complicity. He was not a rural Iago, evilly turning people against one another. But as he became an upstanding householder and father in someone else's name, he could never acknowledge his lie and never give them a chance to pardon him. In this way a deep uneasiness, uncertainty, and wariness would inevitably grow in village and family relations. When people began to wonder publicly about his identity, they also began to suspect him again of magic. And now there was much more fear behind the allegation than when it was made about him during his youth.

For Arnaud, his lie would create a disturbing inner distance between him and other villagers. I have argued that he was not just an impostor trying to take Martin Guerre's money and run. Much of what the Basque Pierre Guerre dreaded in the new Martin's selling of parcels of the *propres* and demanding the accounts can be interpreted otherwise—and must have been by his Artigat supporters—as an acceptable, innovative form of peasant behavior in Languedoc. What the new Martin wanted to do was to stay, to come back, as he did from every trip, to Bertrande's marriage bed. His asking for the accounts was a sign of how comfortable he felt in his role. But in his head there must always have been an out, not the out that gives a creative release from one's fellows and allows reintegration ("I am a Christian and can rise above all this") or allows at least insight and survival ("I am a Basque and this is not really my country"), but a shameful out ("I have no genuine obligation to these people").

For Bertrande, who knew the truth, there were yet other consequences of the lie. She had tried to fashion her life as best she could, using all the leeway and imagination she had as a woman. But she was also proud of her honor and her virtue and was, as she would say later in court, God-fearing. She wanted to live as a mother and family woman at the center of village society. She wanted her son to inherit. Would God punish them because of the lie? And if their marriage were only an invention, was she a shameful adulteress in her mother's eyes and in those of the other village women? And would her daughter Bernarde be stained, since it was said that a child conceived in adultery was marked with the sins of its parents?[17] She loved the new Martin, but he had tricked her once; might he after all not trick her again? And what if the other Martin Guerre came back?

During the rest of the day after the new Martin had been hastened off to prison in Rieux, Bertrande was put under great pressure from her mother and her stepfather. They even threatened to throw her out of the house if she did not formally approve Pierre's action. The stubborn woman calculated and made her plans. She would go along with the court case against the impostor and hope to lose it. She would follow the strategy she had worked out with the new Martin about testimony and hope that the judge would declare him her husband. But given all her doubts and the close calls of the past few months, she would also be prepared to win the case, however terrible the consequences for the new Martin. During the day she sent clothing and money off to the prisoner in Rieux. That evening after dark she approved the actions Pierre Guerre had undertaken as her agent, and rendered herself as plaintiff before the judge of Rieux against the man who had assumed the person of Martin Guerre, her true husband.[18]

7

The Trial at Rieux

⋯•━━◆▶━━•⋯

THE COURT OF Rieux was certainly not unknown to the families of Artigat. There were always disputes that could not be settled locally and ended up there in litigation: Jehanard Loze sued the absentee bishop of Rieux for payment on an annual pension owed the parish; peasants sued each other over the possession of a piece of land; Jeanne de Banquels found herself at odds there with another heiress.[1] When the case of Martin Guerre began, many of the people who testified in it had some notion of the costs and dangers of the king's justice as well as of its potential benefits.

The judge himself received only a middling sum among the salaries paid out to the magistrates dependent on the Parlement of Toulouse. But in the world of Rieux he was an important figure, competing successfully for prestige and power with the local seigniors. In 1560 Firmin Vayssière may already have had the post; a licentiate in law and a staunch Catholic, he was later in charge of investigating Huguenot attacks on church property in the diocese.[2] Together with the king's attorney at Rieux and lawyers in the court, the judge faced one of the most puzzling cases of his career.

Taking on someone else's name and person with intention to defraud was thought a serious crime in sixteenth-century France. There was no fixed penalty for it, but once the king's attorney had joined the case with the "civil party," as Bertrande de Rols was called, the accused was threatened with more than fines. If convicted, he might be sentenced to physical punishment and even death. Here, where the honor and life of a man were at stake, the proof was supposed to be "certain, indubitable, and clearer than day."[3] But how, in a time without photographs, with few portraits, without tape recorders, without fingerprinting,* without identity cards, without birth certificates, with parish records still irregular if kept at all — how did one establish a person's identity beyond doubt? You could test the man's memory, though there was always the possibility that he had been coached. You could ask witnesses to identify him, and hope that they were accurate and truthful. You could consider special marks on his face and body, but their significance could only be established by witnesses who recollected the earlier person. You could look to see whether he resembled other members of the family. You could check his handwriting, but only if he and the earlier person could both write and you had samples of the latter's work. The court of Rieux had to try to extract some kind of truth from such evidence, and henceforth the discourse of the villagers about Martin Guerre would be bent to its purposes.

The first step was to collect information from the witnesses named by the civil party, a list undoubtedly drawn up by both Bertrande and Pierre.[4] (Pierre would have listed

---

*Even with fingerprints, there can be dispute, as shown by the celebrated Giulio Canella case in Turin in 1927–1931. Fingerprints showed the disputed man to be the printer Mario Bruneri, but the wife of Professor Canella claimed nonetheless that he was her husband. Leonardo Sciascia, *Il teatro della memoria* (Turin, 1981).

persons he hoped would support the accusation, Bertrande those she hoped might cast doubt upon it.) To save on the costs, which had to be paid from the purse of the civil party, most of the depositions were probably taken in Artigat or nearby rather than at Rieux. One can imagine the flurry when the judge or his agent appeared on the scene, with opinions proffered right and left by the local notaries and by Master Dominique Boëri, bachelor of laws at Le Fossat. The witnesses were sworn to tell the truth and, after they finished, the examiner read back what they had said word for word (or at least this was what he was supposed to do) so that they could change or add to it. Then they signed their names, if they knew how, or made a mark.

Once the king's attorney had a chance to study all this testimony and give his opinion, the judge opened the hearings at Rieux. He summoned the prisoner, and questioned him about the accusations and the life of Martin Guerre, and listened to what he had to say in his own defense. Then he examined Bertrande de Rols, after which he gave another hearing to the accused to see if he could restate what she had said. At this juncture the judge took seriously the prisoner's claim, supported by testimony from those named by the civil party, that Pierre Guerre was forcing Bertrande to bring the suit against her will; she was removed from Pierre's house and lodged elsewhere.*

---

*Coras says that the defendant asked that Bertrande be put "in some house belonging to respectable people" and that this was done (pp. 37, 45). He comments that "formerly" women might be sequestered in a nunnery (p. 38). The diocese of Rieux had four female houses, all quite aristocratic and none located between Artigat and Rieux: the abbey of Salenques near Le Mas-d'Azil and priories at Longages, La Grace-Dieu, and Sainte-Croix-Volvestre (L. H. Cottineau, *Répertoire topo-bibliographique des Abbayes et Prieurés* [Macon, 1935-1939], cols. 1315, 1643, 2183, 2932). There was also a house of Poor Clares at Pamiers. None of these was practical for Bertrande, who was probably lodged first with a trustworthy family at Artigat and, during her testimony at Rieux, with a family there.

The confrontation between the accused and a witness, from Jean
Milles de Souvigny (Ioannes Millaeus), *Praxis Criminis Persequendi*
(Paris, 1541)

Next came the reexamination of the witnesses and their confrontations with the prisoner. (The civil party is still paying the costs.) The judge makes sure the witness stands by what he or she said in the deposition, and the defendant is called. The latter starts off by making his *reproches*, his objections to the witness and his assessment of the witness' credibility, even before he knows what had been said about him. This is his only chance to throw doubt on the character of his accusers, and he must make the most of it. Then the witness' deposition is read aloud, and the defendant challenges it wherever he needs to, giving alibis and asking questions.

Some cases ended right there after the confrontations, so clear to the king's attorney and the judge was the guilt or innocence of the accused. But not the trial of Martin Guerre. The defendant had named witnesses who could support the claims he had made during his hearings and the confrontations. Bertrande had still not dropped her accusation against him, and he was sure he could provide evidence that she was being suborned. Nor was the judge satisfied with the testimony; he wanted to learn more about this enigmatic peasant woman from Artigat, about the reputation of the other witnesses, and about the identity of the prisoner. The king's attorney was instructed to round up the witnesses for the defendant (now it was his turn to pay costs; he would have to deposit the money in advance). A *monitoire* was read with solemn ceremony in the churches of Artigat, Sajas, and their environs, a letter warning anyone who knew the truth about these matters to reveal it to the judge under threat of excommunication. Even the Protestants must have taken this seriously, however much they doubted the priest's powers.[5]

One hundred and fifty people came to Rieux to testify

before the trial was through. In village after village in two
dioceses, people were asking themselves how you could tell
who a man was—a man snatched from the known context of
fields and family and now on display in the court chambers
of Rieux. The witnesses in Artigat were almost all in accord
on one thing only: when the prisoner came into their midst,
he greeted everyone by name and reminded them accurately
of things they had done together in precise circumstances
many years before. Beyond this they disagreed, as did the
witnesses coming from elsewhere. Forty-five people or more
said that the prisoner was Arnaud du Tilh alias Pansette, or
at least not Martin Guerre, since they had eaten and drunk
with one or the other of them since childhood. These included Carbon Barrau, Arnaud du Tilh's maternal uncle
from Le Pin; people Pansette had made contracts with long
ago; and three men who had recognized the prisoner as du
Tilh even while he was living as Bertrande de Rols's husband. About thirty to forty people said that the defendant
was surely Martin Guerre; they had known him since the
cradle. These included Martin's four sisters, his two brothers-in-law, and Catherine Boëri from one of the most re-
spected families in the locality.

Those witnesses who had known Martin Guerre before he
left Artigat stretched their memories twelve years back.
Peasants might be expected to have good visual memories—
there are many sights, shapes, and colors that they have to
keep in mind in the course of their work—but here again
there was disagreement. Some witnesses maintained that
Martin had been taller, thinner, and darker than the accused, had a flatter nose and more projecting lower lip and a
scar on his eyebrow that was nowhere to be seen on this
impostor. The shoemaker told his story about the different
shoe sizes, Martin's larger than the prisoner's. Other wit-

nesses insisted that Martin Guerre had extra teeth in his jaw, a scar on his forehead, three warts on his right hand; and each of these was discovered on the prisoner.

Finally, there was a large group of witnesses, around sixty or more, who refused to identify the prisoner one way or another. Perhaps they feared some retribution if they took a position, a calumny suit from the defendant if he should be declared innocent or trouble with Pierre Guerre. But what they said publicly was more straightforward: the prisoner really did resemble Martin Guerre, despite all the testimony about lip, eyebrow, and nose. They were not sure who he was and, in a case of such consequence, how could they presume to make a judgment?[6]

During these weeks, the woman who was seeking a judgment had a difficult and lonely time. She was living in unfamiliar surroundings away from the new Martin, who must have been wondering about her loyalty. Her mother and stepfather were hoping that this case would leave the deceiver dead or at least in the galleys; her sisters-in-law were no doubt asking themselves why she had brought the complaint at all. The honor of Bertrande de Rols had become the subject of a monitory letter read from pulpits in the Lèze valley and beyond. And in her testimony she had to be cagey; she must say only what the defendant had learned in the past about Martin Guerre so that he could not be tripped up in his answers, but nothing that could leave her open to a charge of adultery. She had to manipulate the image of the woman-easily-deceived, a skill that women often displayed before officers of justice any time it was to their advantage.[7]

Possibly Bertrande had the chance to talk to an attorney before the hearings at Rieux, but in the presence of the judge, his clerk, and the king's attorney, she was on her own. It was hard to present herself in this man's world, even for a woman who held her head high and spoke her mind in the village. But she answered the judge's questions about the life of Martin Guerre, from the too-early marriage to the young man's departure, and then she volunteered some new details. The court must hear about the impotence of Martin Guerre and how it ended, and about an even more private moment between them. They had been at a wedding long ago and for lack of marriage beds (*cubilia*), Bertrande had to spend the night with her cousin; by agreement, Martin crept into the bed after the other woman had fallen asleep. (Le Sueur stops his account here, but Bertrande did not, going on to tell "the things they had done before, during, and after the secret act of marriage."[8])

Bertrande played her double role perfectly, until her confrontation with the prisoner. It was a delicate situation for him too, and he had to raise objections to her credibility with care: she was "a respectable woman and honest" who told the truth, except when she said he was an impostor; in that she was being coerced to lie by Pierre Guerre. He then made a test of her love and expressed his own, saying to the judge that if she would take an oath that he was not her husband Martin Guerre, he would submit to any death the court chose. And Bertrande was silent.[9]

If the wife of Martin Guerre was divided, the new Martin seemed never so whole as during the trials. On center stage, all his wits tuned to proving who he was, he never missed a step in any recollection, whether it was describing the clothes that individual guests wore at Martin Guerre's wedding or telling how he sneaked into bed with Bertrande and her cousin in the dark of the night. He bubbled with details about his activities in France and Spain after he had left Artigat, giving names of persons who would confirm his account (the court checked and they did). His assessment of the witnesses in his confrontations must have been unusually good—"vivement et vallablement reprochez," said Coras later in evaluating the challenges to Carbon Barrau and others "who gave in such detail facts which weigh against the prisoner."[10] What he said we can only imagine. To Carbon Barrau, perhaps, "I've never seen this man before in my life. And if he is my uncle, why can't he produce other members of the family who say so?" To the shoemaker: "This man is a drinking companion of Pierre Guerre. Let him show his records about the size of my feet. And who else can support his lies?"

All of this seems to have been done by the defendant without benefit of legal advice. The ordinance of Villars-Cotteret of 1539 had made it possible to deny the right of counsel to the accused in a criminal trial, though recent research is showing that it was not often invoked.[11] A lawyer would have been in his element advising the new Martin, for his case bristled with issues on which he might have held up proceedings and appealed, from his armed arrest before daybreak on. But the trial took only a few months, despite the monitory letter and all the witnesses. One suspects that the prisoner, with his cleverness and good ear, quickly picked up the kinds of arguments that would make an impression on men trained in the law. The accused centered his defense on one issue: Pierre Guerre's hatred of him because of his suit over the property. Having failed to kill him, he and his sons-in-law had hatched this plot against him, even inventing a new kind of crime, imposture. "If ever a husband was ill treated by his close relatives, it was certainly he—and unjustly."[12] He should be freed and Pierre

Guerre punished as a calumniator with the same harsh penalty that he, Martin, would receive for fraud.*

After the last group of witnesses was heard, the king's attorney pressed for a final sentence. The evidence was hard to evaluate, and the judge's request for a report on the defendant's resemblance to the sisters and son of Martin Guerre made matters no clearer. The prisoner did not resemble Sanxi; he did resemble the sisters. The handwriting test could not be used because if by chance the defendant could now write his name (and it was the small group of rural merchants who were virtually the only villagers other than notaries and priests who could sign their contracts), neither Pansette nor Martin Guerre had ever done so in earlier days.

The court might have considered passing a sentence to torture the defendant to see if he would confess: for that to be done, the law required strong evidence of his guilt from the testimony of one irreproachable witness or circumstantial evidence from two witnesses. But the judge of Rieux did not bother with it. Perhaps he thought it would be unsuccessful (and new research on the Parlement of Paris is showing that torture did not yield a confession very often). Perhaps he thought he had a good enough case without a confession, and that this defendant would simply appeal the sentence of torture to the Parlement of Toulouse.[13]

Be that as it may, the judge declared the defendant guilty of taking on the name and person of Martin Guerre and abusing Bertrande de Rols. The civil party had demanded

---

*Coras justified this law of the talion in his annotation (p. 35), but the criminal judge Jean Imbert in his contemporary handbook of judicial practice said that it was no longer in effect. Persons condemned for calumnious accusation were usually punished with a formal ceremony of apology and a fine. Considering the current abuse of accusation, Imbert sometimes wished the law of talion was back in use. Jean Imbert, *Institutions Forenses, ou practique iudiciaire* (Poitiers, 1563), pp. 446, 498.

that he beg her pardon in a public ceremony and pay her 2000 livres as well as her costs for the trial. The king's attorney asked for death, which superseded Bertrande's request. This was not too surprising: in 1557 the Sénéchaussée of Lyon had condemned two men to be hanged for making false contracts in another man's name for only a few months. The judge of Rieux sentenced the prisoner to be beheaded and quartered—a curious compliment, for beheading was supposed to be reserved for nobles.[14]

The condemned man appealed immediately to the Parlement of Toulouse, protesting his innocence. Shortly afterward he was taken to that city under guard and at his own expense. The great pile of papers generated by the case came along with him, paid for by Bertrande. On April 30, 1560, the Criminal Chamber of the Parlement already had before it the case of "Martin Guerre, prisoner in the Conciergerie."[15]

8

The Trial at Toulouse

·····━━◀◈▶━━·····

THE PARLEMENT OF TOULOUSE was in the one hundred
and seventeenth year of its existence, its buildings reno-
vated and the numbers of its officeholders increasing. The
power of that body in Languedoc was very great indeed.In
1560 it was not only judging civil and criminal cases on appeal and sometimes in the first instance, and keeping a
watch on the activities of the lower courts in its region, but
also deciding what to do about anti-Catholic image breakers
in Toulouse and sending commissioners out to investigate
illegal assemblies and weapon carrying, heresies, and mur-
ders in the diocese of Lombez. Its presidents and judges
were a wealthy and well-educated elite, owning fine houses
in Toulouse and estates in the country and acquiring titles
of nobility by one means or another. Their judicial robes
were becoming more splendid, and they were addressed in
terms of respect and honor: "integerrimus, amplissimus,
meritissimus," says Jean de Coras of one of them in a dedication written before he had joined their ranks; "eruditissimus
et aequissimus" of another; and of the whole Parlement,
"gravissimus sanctissimusque Senatus."[1]

The Criminal Chamber, or La Tournelle as it was called,
was one of the five chambers of the Parlement and made up

of a rotating group of ten to eleven judges and two or three presidents. Those who happened to be sitting on it for the appeal of "Martin Guerre" included some of the luminaries of the court. There was the learned Jean de Coras, with all his legal publications. There was Michel Du Faur, former judge in the Sénéchaussée and now a president of the Parlement; from a family of distinguished men of the law, he was married to a Bernuy, whose dowry came from profits in the Toulouse pastel-dye trade. Jean de Mansencal himself, the first president of the Parlement, came down from the high chamber for the last days of the trial. Owner of a splendid Renaissance house in the city, he also had property in the diocese of Lombez, not far from the village where Arnaud du Tilh was born.

Linked by their work and even by marriage (the daughter of judge Etienne de Bonald would shortly marry Mansencal's son), the men assigned to La Tournelle in 1560 were also beginning to sense strong differences among them. Three of the judges soon emerged as strong Protestants—Jean de Coras, François de Ferrières, and Pierre Robert—and a few others, such as Michel Du Faur, were at least sympathetic to the Reformed cause. On the other side, Mansencal was a loyal Catholic and the more intransigent president Jean Daffis and Nicholas Latomy later used every means at their disposal to stamp out the new heresy.[2]

For the time, though, they could share an interest in the curious case that had come up to them from the court of Rieux. They had all had years of experience in the Parlement—old Simon Reynier had been hearing cases for almost forty years, and Jean de Coras, the last appointed, had been a judge since 1553—but had they ever considered the case of a wife who claimed that she had mistaken another man for her husband for more than three years? Adultery, concubines, bigamy, yes, but a husband who was an impostor? The Chamber decided that Jean de Coras would be the reporter for the proceedings, which meant that he would look closely into the issues and finally prepare a report on all the arguments and make a recommendation for the sentence. François de Ferrières was commissioned to help him in his inquiries and in questioning witnesses. To start with, the court would hear Bertrande de Rols, who had asked to appear, and Pierre Guerre as well.[3]

While these two were making their way from Artigat to Toulouse, the man still insisting that he was Martin Guerre was sitting with his legs in chains in the Conciergerie. This was no special treatment; the escape rate from the Conciergerie had been so high that all the men there except debtors and those owing fines were in chains unless they were very ill. He was free to talk to anyone within earshot, and we can imagine him, with his irrepressible tongue, regaling the men who were in prison with him: an alleged kidnapper from Carcassonne; a notary, a priest, and a spurmaker from Pamiers, all accused of heresy; and two mysterious men claiming to be from "Astaraps in Little Egypt."[4]

In early May Bertrande and Pierre were heard, and then before the whole Chamber they each had their confrontation with the defendant. There seems to have been no problem with language: the trial was supposed to be conducted "in the vernacular of the area," and all the members of the court were from the region. Bertrande began with a statement intended to convince the judges that she had never been the prisoner's accomplice; she knew that her honor had been stained, but it was all because of the traps laid for her by other people. She spoke with trepidation, her eyes fixed on the floor ("defixis in terram oculis satis trepidè"). The prisoner then addressed her with animation ("alacriori vultu") and affection, saying that he wanted no harm to come to her and that he knew this whole affair had been staged by his uncle. He showed a face "so assured," comments Coras, "and so much more so than the said de Rols that there were few judges present who were not persuaded that the prisoner was the true husband and that the imposture came from the side of the wife and the uncle." After the two confrontations, the Criminal Chamber ordered Pierre and Bertrande both to be imprisoned, Pierre presumably not too close to "Martin Guerre" and Bertrande in the section of the Conciergerie reserved for women.[5]

Now there resumed the telling and retelling of the life of Martin Guerre. Coras and Ferrières interviewed Bertrande first. If she had wanted to betray him at this point, all she had to do was tell a story he could not repeat; instead she adhered to the text they had agreed upon months before. Then many times over they questioned the defendant, trying in vain to trick him into a mistake.* Coras reported:

> His remarks sustained at length and containing so many true signs, gave great occasion to the judges to be persuaded of the innocence [of the defendant], and beyond that to admire the felicity of his memory, for he recounted innumerable events that happened more than twenty years before. The commissioners by every means possible tried to surprise him in some lie, but could get no advantage on him nor induce him to respond other than truthfully in all things.[6]

Witnesses would have to be questioned, that was clear, and some twenty-five to thirty were heard by the commis-

---

*"It is sometimes permissible for Judges to lie," a judge of the Parlement of Toulouse was later to write, "in order to uncover the truth about crimes and felonies." Bernard de La Roche-Flavin, *Treize livres des Parlemens de France* (Geneva, 1621), book 8, ch. 39.

sioners, chosen both from those who had already testified and from those who had not. Again there were confrontations with the defendant—Carbon Barrau wept when he saw the prisoner in chains—but "Martin Guerre" made his challenges to him as he had done before. Some seven witnesses were summoned to Toulouse at the end of May specifically to have confrontations with Bertrande. In the shameful situation of being a prisoner herself, she had to face her sister-in-law Jeanne Guerre and important men from the Lèze valley such as Jean Loze and Jean Banquels, who presumably gave testimony bearing on whether she had been suborned.[7]

Over the summer of 1560 Jean de Coras sifted through all this evidence and decided what he should say in a report. It may have been a relief to spend his time on Martin Guerre. His *De iuris Arte*, a major treatise, had appeared earlier in the year, and he was not yet at work on anything new. Meanwhile the political situation in France was disquieting in the wake of the failed Protestant conspiracy of Amboise a few months before, and Toulouse itself was full of confrontations between supporters of the new religion and supporters of the old. Some days when the Criminal Chamber was sentencing heretics, he just stayed away.[8] He knew where the truth lay there and was not yet ready to put all his public force behind it. It was easier for the moment to find out the truth about a man's identity.

The additional testimony from witnesses turned out to add very little: nine or ten people were sure the prisoner was Martin Guerre, seven or eight said he was Arnaud du Tilh, and the rest said they did not know. Coras embarked upon a systematic analysis of the witnesses and their testimony; this he must have found wanting in the judgment at Rieux. The weight of numbers from the two trials argued against the defendant. What counted, however, was not the number of witnesses testifying to an identity, but the quality of those witnesses—whether they were people of integrity, doing their best to tell the truth, or whether they spoke merely from passion, fear, or interest—and the likelihood of their testimony. For this particular case Coras thought the testimony of close relatives was of the highest value*. They should be most likely to recognize a man "because of the closeness of blood" and because they had grown up with him. But here he found relatives making positive identification on both sides.

To condemn a person, a court must have proof that a crime has really been committed and that the accused is the person who did it. Even a confession standing alone was not sufficient to establish these two facts, for a defendant might not confess the truth, with or without torture. In any case, there was no confession here. Could proof be established by the traditional rule requiring the testimony about observed acts by two witnesses worthy of credence? Coras had some precise facts attested to, but there were problems each time. For example, Pelegrin de Liberos swore that the defendant had responded to the name Arnaud du Tilh and had given him two handkerchiefs for his brother Jean; but he was the only witness so to depose and he was effectively challenged by the defendant. Two people testified that they had heard the soldier from Rochefort announce that Martin Guerre had lost a leg at the battle of Saint-Quentin, but because it was only "hearsay" this could not carry full weight.

The tangible evidence, taken into consideration in sixteenth-century criminal cases even though it was not part of the medieval theory of how proof was established, also did

---

*See below, p. 85, on the general question of the testimony of close relatives in a criminal case and on the brothers of Arnaud du Tilh.

not yield any clear-cut answers. Much of it rested on the testimony of people who recollected what Martin Guerre looked like, and perhaps they were lying or simply betrayed by memory. Those who claimed that the prisoner had the same marks and scars as Martin Guerre had each picked on a different wart or fingernail; no two testified to the same mark. On the other hand, if it were true that the young Martin Guerre had thinner legs than the defendant, experience often showed that people who were slender in their youth became heavier as they advanced in age. That the accused knew almost no Basque could mean that he was not Martin Guerre because it was not likely "that a native Basque would not know how to speak his language," or it could simply mean that having left Labourd so young he had never really learned his parents' tongue.[9]

Coras was "in great perplexity," but the reporter had to make a recommendation. The more he reflected on the evidence, the more likely it seemed that the defendant was who he said he was and that the sentence of the judge of Rieux should be reversed.

He considered the evidence about Bertrande. She was a woman who had lived "virtuously and honorably," so information produced by the monitory letter had confirmed. She had shared her bed with the prisoner for more than three years, "during which long interval it is not likely that the said de Rols would not have recognized him for a stranger if the prisoner had not been truly Martin Guerre." She had insisted for months that he was her husband in opposition to her stepfather and her mother, even protecting him from harm with her own body, and had received him in her bed only a few hours before signing the complaint. Then, before the judge of Rieux, she had refused to swear that he was not Martin Guerre. This added nothing one way or the other to the truth of the matter, for in criminal cases "the proof by oath is not legitimate." But it did indicate her state of mind, and this impression was reinforced by her uncertain and nervous manner during the confrontation with the defendant before the Criminal Chamber in May. It seemed probable, as Bertrande had earlier been heard to claim herself, that she had been coerced into bringing a false accusation.[10]

He considered Pierre Guerre. One wonders what went on when the jurist from Réalmont had his hearings with the elderly Artigat tilemaker with his Basque accent. How did the uncle express his anger and sense of grievance against the impostor, and since Coras was using "manner" as an index of the good faith of his witnesses, how did this influence his recommendation that Pierre Guerre be clapped into chains? At any rate, the evidence he had before him did not put the man in a good light. The litigation about the accounts and its outcome were on record, providing a strong motive for a false accusation. Pierre himself had confessed to misrepresenting himself as Bertrande's agent before the judge of Rieux. His conspiracy with his wife and his sons-in-law to have the defendant killed had been described by "several witnesses," including the reputable Jean Loze. This was sufficient proof to warrant an order to torture Pierre Guerre to see if he would confess to attempted murder, calumnious accusation, and the suborning of testimony from Bertrande de Rols. Indeed, Le Sueur claims that the Criminal Chamber was considering such a step, though it never got to the point of passing the sentence. Whatever the case, Coras viewed false accusation as a grave and too frequent crime, a deliberate plan to do evil to one's neighbor against God's eighth commandment.[11]

Finally there was the accused. Much evidence argued in

his favor. Coras considered the four sisters of Martin Guerre to be exceptionally good witnesses, "as respectable and honest women as there are in Gascony, who have always maintained that the prisoner was surely their brother Martin Guerre." (Their support may have looked especially disinterested to Coras, for they would have even less chance to inherit Guerre properties if Martin Guerre had yet another son.) That the defendant resembled them seemed more telling than his lack of resemblance to Sanxi, Coras said, for he was closer to them in age, while Sanxi was only a boy of thirteen. There was also the tested fact of the prisoner's assured and perfect recall of everything about the life of Martin Guerre, including the intimate details presented by the plaintiff herself. The reports that Arnaud du Tilh had been dissolute, "given over to every kind of wickedness," did not harm the prisoner's case; if anything, they helped it, for he did not appear to be that kind of man.

A decision for the defendant would give expression to the principle of Roman law "that it was better to leave unpunished a guilty person than to condemn an innocent one." More important, it would give weight to a preference in the civil law which was taken very seriously by the courts in sixteenth-century France: it would favor marriage and the children issuing from it. "In situations where there is some doubt," said Coras, "the support either of marriage or of children ... shifts the balance." Bertrande would have a husband; Sanxi and Bernarde a father.[12]

The Criminal Chamber was about to make its final judgment of the case, opinions being "more disposed to the advantage of the prisoner and against the said Pierre Guerre and de Rols,"[13] when a man with a wooden leg appeared at the buildings of the Parlement of Toulouse. He said his name was Martin Guerre.

[handwritten margin note: Hollywood moment.]

9

The Return of Martin Guerre

AFTER MARTIN GUERRE had his leg shot off at the battle of Saint-Quentin, he had two pieces of good fortune. First, he did not die of his wound, but survived the surgeon's treatment and was able to hobble around on a wooden leg. Second, his masters, either Pedro de Mendoza or his brother, the Cardinal, asked Philip II to assist Martin in his reduced circumstances. The king rewarded him for his service to Spain by a position for life as a lay brother in one of the houses of the military order of Saint John of Jerusalem. This order was the strictest in the country in requiring proofs of nobility for its knights; the bankers of Burgos begged in vain to have the rules bent for them.[1] Martin Guerre carried on as before, a small part of an all-male world dominated by aristocrats.

Why did he ever decide, after an absence of twelve years, to cross the Pyrenees on his wooden leg and come back to his old life? This is the greatest mystery in the story of Martin Guerre. Coras says nothing about his reasons, though he suggests that Martin discovered the imposture only after his return. Le Sueur claims that he went first to Artigat when he arrived, heard what had happened, and left immediately with Sanxi for Toulouse. There are problems with Le Sueur's account, however, for it makes it difficult to explain the sisters' surprise in the last days of the trial.

Still it is conceivable that Martin Guerre returned by chance, just in the nick of time. He could have wearied of the restricted activity of a religious house and, layman that he was, decided that it was better to live with his impairment in the bosom of his family, where he might have some authority. The peace of Cāteau-Cambrésis had been signed by Spain, France, and England the year before, and the cardinal of Burgos had been assigned by Philip II to meet his bride Elisabeth de Valois at the French border in December 1559. Martin Guerre might hope that in this time of reconciliation he would be pardoned for his soldiering for Spain.[2]

More likely, I think, is that he heard of the trial before his return. Pierre Guerre would certainly have hoped to get news to him, if he were still alive. The case was being discussed in villages throughout Languedoc, and the judge of Rieux had sent investigators as far as Spain to check the testimony of the new Martin about his visit there. The burghers of Toulouse and lawyers from elsewhere were also talking about the affair, even though the judges were not supposed to reveal their deliberations to anyone outside the court and the public was not allowed to attend the trial until the final sentencing. Word also might have been passed to the original Martin Guerre through the order of Saint John of Jerusalem, for it had several houses in Languedoc and the county of Foix.[3]

Who am I, Martin Guerre might have asked himself, if another man has lived out the life I left behind and is in the process of being declared the heir of my father Sanxi, the husband of my wife, and the father of my son? The original Martin Guerre may have come back to repossess his identity, his persona, before it was too late.

Once he got to Toulouse about late July, he was placed in the custody of the guard of the Parlement, and hearings began. "Newcomer!" the defendant is said to have shouted when his confrontation began with the man from Spain, "evildoer, rascal! This man has been bought for cash and has been instructed by Pierre Guerre." At the last minute he had arrived to trouble the holy estate of matrimony; the accused would unmask him or be willing to be hanged. And, strange to behold, the man with the wooden leg remembered events in the house of Martin Guerre less well than the prisoner.[4]

It was a moment of triumph for the person who had once been called Pansette. It would be a mistake to interpret his behavior that day and in the next few weeks as simply a desperate attempt to stay alive. Live or dead, he was defending the identity he had fashioned for himself against a stranger. (The reader will recall that it is most likely that the two men never met before.)

Coras and Ferrières had ten or twelve more hearings separately with the two men, asked the newcomer "hidden" questions on subjects not broached before, verified his answers, then discovered that the defendant could respond just about as well. The accused seemed to have an air of magic about him. Trying to take him off guard, President de Mansencal asked him how he had invoked the evil spirit that taught him so much about the people of Artigat. Coras said that he paled and for once hesitated, to the judge a sure sign of guilt.[5] This reaction, I think, may have resulted not only from the defendant's sense of danger, but also from anger that his natural skills were being so misrepresented.

The Criminal Chamber then moved on to a final set of confrontations. Carbon Barrau was called once again and this time also Arnaud du Tilh's brothers, thereby violating (as was increasingly the case in the sixteenth century) a medieval rule that brothers could not bear witness against each other in a criminal case. The du Tilhs fled rather than come to Toulouse.

For Pierre Guerre, haggard from his months in prison, the commissioners arranged a theatrical test. The newcomer was placed among a group of men all dressed alike. Pierre recognized his nephew, wept, and rejoiced that at last his fortune was changing.

For the sisters, called in separately, the two Martins were placed side by side. After studying the one-legged man for a while, Jeanne said, "This is my brother Martin Guerre." She had been deceived all the time by the traitor who resembled him. She hugged Martin, brother and sister wept, and so with the other sisters as well.[6]

It was the turn of Bertrande de Rols. Had her spirits flagged after some three months in the Conciergerie? She had lost weight and been ill, but at least some of the women in prison with her were accused of heresy, which meant the possibility of discussing the Gospel with them. Also present was a propertied woman, who like Bertrande was a plaintiff who had been imprisoned. Yet another prisoner left for a while to give birth.[7] It was a woman's world and may have reminded Bertrande of the years of waiting for Martin Guerre's return. She was sufficiently steeled to the different possible outcomes of her situation so that when she arrived at the Criminal Chamber she was able to play her role quite well.

After one look at the newcomer, she began to tremble and weep (this according to Coras, who considered it the duty of a good judge to note the expressions of his witnesses) and ran to embrace him, asking his pardon for her fault, committed because she had been overwhelmed by the ruses and seductions of Arnaud du Tilh. Out tumbled all the prepared excuses: your sisters believed him too readily; your uncle accepted him; I wanted to have my husband back so much that I believed him, especially when he knew such private things about me; when I realized he was a fraud, I wished I were dead and would have killed myself except that I was afraid of God; the minute I knew he had stolen my honor, I took him to court.

Martin Guerre showed not a single sign of sorrow at the tears of Bertrande de Rols, and with a fierce and severe countenance (assisted perhaps by memories of the Spanish preachers he had been among) said, "Leave aside these tears . . . And don't excuse yourself by my sisters nor my uncle; for there is neither father, mother, uncle, sister, or brother who ought better to know their son, nephew, or brother than the wife ought to know her husband. And for the disaster which has befallen our house, no one is to blame but you." Coras and Ferrières reminded him that he bore some guilt here, having abandoned Bertrande in the first place, but he would not be moved.[8]

Martin Guerre had now been recognized. Even without a confession, the court had sufficient proof for a definitive judgment. Jean de Coras prepared a new report and drafted a sentence; the Criminal Chamber agreed upon a text. Arnaud du Tilh alias Pansette was found guilty of "imposture and false supposition of name and person and of adultery."[9] Despite the suspicion of magic and diabolic invocation in the last weeks of the trial, this was not mentioned in the sentence. Du Tilh was condemned to perform an *amende honorable*, a public apology, and then to be put to death in Artigat.

The penalty probably required some discussion among the judges. A term in prison was not one of the possibilities for Arnaud du Tilh, of course, for prisons were only for people awaiting trial and convicted debtors. The choice lay among fines, various kinds of physical punishment (whipping, branding, mutilation), banishment, a term rowing in the king's galleys, and death. For this case Coras could find virtually no texts in French law to provide guidance; "supposition of name and person" was treated little outside the limited case of forging a signature. The ancient texts varied

The first pictorial representation of the case, showing the couple as of higher station than they were. From Jacob Cats, *Alle de Wercken* (Amsterdam, 1658)

widely, some treating imposture as a game that need not be punished, others assigning a mild punishment, others banishment, a very few death. In 1532 a royal edict had made possible the death penalty for "the multitude" of people drawing up false contracts and making false depositions before the courts, but judicial practice was not uniform. Coras may have heard what had happened in 1557 to the appeal of two Lyon impostors (the ones signing contracts as Michel Mure) from their sentence of death by the Sénéchaussée of Lyon: the Parlement of Paris moderated their punishment to whipping and nine years in the galleys. The next time the Sénéchaussée had to sentence an impostor, the Greek Citracha who collected the debts owed a dead man, it condemned him to restore all the sums wrongly taken, to pay 500 livres to the king, and to be banished from France.[10]

Du Tilh's was a more serious crime, however. It involved stealing a heritage, which could be compared to a woman's misrepresenting her illegitimate child to her husband as his own so that the child could inherit. More important, he had committed adultery, a crime that Coras thought should be punished more severely and consistently in general. The Parlement of Toulouse was handing out death penalties for adultery only where social obligation had been sharply violated, as in 1553, when a judge's clerk was condemned to be hanged for sleeping with his master's wife, and in 1556, when a landowner's wife was convicted of adultery with her sharecropper (both were hanged).[11]

Out of these considerations came the choice of the death sentence for Arnaud, a choice for which at least one man of the law was later to take the court to task. He would not be beheaded though, as the judge of Rieux had prescribed, but hanged, as befitted a mere commoner who was a dissolute betrayer. The court would not go so far as to burn him alive, but because of his detestable crime his corpse would be burned "so that the memory of so miserable and abominable a person would disappear completely and be lost."

In a few ways the Criminal Chamber treated the interests of Arnaud du Tilh with consideration, a tactic that made things easier for Martin Guerre and Bertrande de Rols but that also shows some lingering respect for the man who had dazzled them with his testimony. His daughter Bernarde was found to be legitimate, the court deciding to accept Bertrande's claim that she thought she was having intercourse with Martin Guerre when the child was conceived. Here there was ample precedent. For a child to be a bastard, both parents had to be conscious of the circumstances; the children of a woman unaware that she had married a priest would be legitimate.

More unusual, the court did not confiscate the goods and properties of Arnaud du Tilh in the diocese of Lombez and turn them over to the king, as was done most of the time with a criminal condemned to death. Instead, after Bertrande had been reimbursed for her expenses for the trial, the goods would pass to their child Bernarde.[12]

Furthermore, the condemned man was not sentenced to be tortured before his execution so as to induce him to name his accomplices, what was called being given "la question préalable." Coras did recommend torture on some occasions; earlier in 1560 he and President Daffis had signed a sentence providing that a certain Jean Thomas alias Le Provincial "will be put to the question to know from his mouth the truth about the abuses, crimes, and evil spells imputed to him."[13] But the Criminal Chamber may have

thought that the astonishing Arnaud was unlikely to break
—and if he did, they certainly did not want him to name
Bertrande de Rols as his accomplice at the last minute.

For the Chamber had to decide what to do about the
woman prisoner in the Conciergerie. What could one say
about the beautiful wife so easily deceived and so obstinate
in her error? After much discussion, the judges agreed to
accept her good faith; the female sex was, after all, fragile.
She would not be prosecuted for fraud, bigamy, or adultery
(a penalty for the last in these circumstances might have
placed her in a convent until her husband decided he would
take her back), and her daughter would be legitimate.

So too with Martin Guerre. The court spent a long time
deciding whether charges should be made against him for
having deserted his family for so many years and for having
fought for the enemies of France. They finally decided that
his departure could be attributed to his youth, "the heat
and levity of youth, which was then boiling up in him,"
and that his serving Philip II could be blamed on his masters, whom as a lackey he was bound to obey, rather than on
any desire "to offend his natural prince." Given what had
happened to his leg, to his goods, and to his wife, he had
been punished enough.

Nor would Pierre Guerre be prosecuted for his wrongful
representation of himself as Bertrande's agent or for his
scheme to murder Arnaud du Tilh. He had already risked
goods and even his life in pushing the case against the impostor: if it had been lost—as it almost was—he would have
faced a heavy penalty for false accusation before a court of
law.[14]

Everything in the court's final judgment was intended to
enforce the criteria that Coras had been using earlier to justify a sentence in favor of the new Martin: it supported

marriage and the children issuing from it. On September 11, President de Mansencal summoned Bertrande de Rols, Martin Guerre, and Arnaud du Tilh to appear before the whole Chamber. Pansette insisted he was Martin Guerre, no matter what the president said. Mansencal then tried to reconcile Bertrande and Martin, rebuking them for their faults and urging them to forget the past. The defendant interrupted him repeatedly, challenging every word.

It was the new Martin's poorest performance—or else his sincerest. He had lost, and it was now his turn to be the jealous husband. To the court he came across as impudent and petulant, and accordingly it made a last-minute change in the sentence.[15] It was intended that he make two formal apologies, one before the Chamber, one at Artigat. He would now have to do only the latter. Who knew what he would say before the court?*

On September 12, the Parlement opened its doors so that the public could hear the sentencing. A huge crowd pushed into the courtroom; in their midst seems to have been young Michel de Montaigne, now a judge at the Parlement of Bordeaux.[16] Mansencal read the decree absolving Martin Guerre, Bertrande de Rols, and Pierre Guerre and denying the appeal of Arnaud du Tilh alias Pansette, "calling himself Martin Guerre." He would start his public apology in front of the church of Artigat and then be led through the village and executed before the house of Martin Guerre. The judge of Rieux would take charge of the affair. Coras did not

---

*Coras's account of this is very strange. Why punish Arnaud du Tilh's misbehavior by lifting one of the apologies? Would it not have been more appropriate to change the apology before the court to a more humiliating one before the village? Either Coras is misrepresenting what happened, or we have here another example of the mixed feelings of the judges toward the extraordinary Arnaud du Tilh.

record the expression on the faces of Bertrande de Rols and Arnaud du Tilh.

———◆———

Four days later the gibbet had been built in front of the house in which Bertrande's marriage bed had been installed some twenty-two years before. The family was all back from Toulouse, and people had come from miles around to see the impostor and witness the execution. The village was no longer divided as it had been for a year or more. The lie was in the open now, and the ritual would begin by which the liar would be humiliated, seek pardon, and be cast out.

Pansette did his best to make it a memorable occasion. He began the day by taking back his old name. He volunteered his confession to the judge of Rieux, starting with his being hailed as Martin Guerre by the two men at Mane. Everything had been done by natural means, his and those of certain accomplices, whom he named*. Nothing was due to magic. Bertrande's role he concealed from start to finish. According to Coras (though not to Le Sueur), he also confessed to several petty thefts in his youth.

Then like any good peasant father he made his testament. He listed all his debtors and creditors in money, wool, grain, wine, and millet and requested that they be paid from the properties he had inherited from Arnaud Guilhem du

---

*Coras says only that he confessed that "some people had given him secret information and advice" (p. 83). Le Sueur says he named "two people" who had helped him (*Admiranda historia de Pseudo Martino* ... [Lyon, 1561], p. 22). Perhaps they were the two friends of the missing man who had first mistaken him for Martin.

Tilh and others; they were currently being occupied by Carbon Barrau. To make sure that his uncle paid, he started a civil suit against him, presumably to be carried on by his executors. His daughter Bernarde—now Bernarde du Tilh—he made his universal heir; his brother Jean du Tilh of Le Pin and a certain Dominique Rebendaire of Toulouse were to be her guardians and the executors of his will.

The *amende honorable* started with the condemned man on his knees in front of the church in the traditional garb of the penitent—white shirt, bare head, and bare feet, with a torch in his hands. He asked pardon of God, the king, the court, Martin Guerre and Bertrande de Rols, and Pierre Guerre. Led through the village with the hangman's rope on his neck, the golden-tongued peasant addressed the crowds. He was the Arnaud du Tilh who had shamelessly and craftily taken the goods of another and the honor of his wife. He commended the judges in Toulouse for their investigation and wished that the honorable Jean de Coras and François de Ferrières could be present to hear him now. Even on the ladder up to the gibbet he was talking, preaching to the man who would take his place not to be harsh with Bertrande. She was a woman of honor, virtue, and constancy, he could attest to it. As soon as she suspected him, she had driven him away. It had taken great courage and spirit to do what she had done. Of Bertrande he asked only that she pardon him. He died asking God for mercy through his son Jesus Christ.[17]

10

The Storyteller

⸺◆⸺

SHORTLY AFTER THE SENTENCING of Arnaud du Tilh, the Parlement of Toulouse recessed for two months, as it did every September. Jean de Coras did not leave immediately for his country home in Réalmont. Instead he went to his study in Toulouse and began to write the story of the man whose burning had been intended to efface his memory forever. By October 1, 1560, he was most of the way through a first draft.[1] Simultaneously, a young man named Guillaume Le Sueur was recording his version of the same events. There was something about the story that touched their own lives, something disturbing and amazing that needed to be told.

It is difficult to detect the appeal of the case for Guillaume Le Sueur, for he is a little-known figure. Born to a wealthy and propertied merchant of Boulogne-sur-Mer in Picardy, Le Sueur was sent off to Toulouse to be trained in the civil law. His brother Pierre became a royal financial officer and by the end of 1561 was using his house in Boulogne for "assemblies and prayers according to the new religion." Guillaume seems to have shared his sentiments and for a time was part of the entourage of the Protestant Prince of Condé. By 1566 he was a lawyer in the Sénéchaussée of the

Boulonnais, several years later its lieutenant of streams and forests. In 1596 he was to write the first history of his native town, a work of some merit. Even before this La Croix du Maine had heard of him, describing him in his *Bibliothèque* of 1584 as "poet in Latin and French." He knew Greek as well, translating the Greek version of the third book of Maccabees into Latin verse for an edition of 1566.

Also to his credit is the "Admirable History of the Pseudo-Martin of Toulouse," which he composed in Latin and which was circulating in that city in manuscript not long after the trial. He dedicated it to Michel Du Faur, fourth president of the Parlement and a member of the Tournelle all during the case of Martin Guerre. As Le Sueur said later in a dedication to Chancellor Michel de L'Hôpital, he had been "adopted into the family and clientele of the Du Faurs, a house surpassing all in the region for its singular erudition, integrity of life, splendor and honor." His evidence on the trial was probably taken from the president's own words and papers—he refers to himself as having "collected" ("colligebat") the story—and perhaps he was present in the court in some minor capacity. What is certain is that in 1560 Guillaume Le Sueur hoped to rise within the world of law and legal rhetorical culture, and that he also had literary and classical interests of his own.[2]

About Jean de Coras we know a great deal. He was illustrious, "clarissimus," as his publishers had been saying about him on his title pages for some time. In the year of the Martin Guerre trial, his own "Life" had appeared, told by a former student, Antoine Usilis, as the preface to Coras's *De iuris Arte*. He was born about 1515 in Réalmont in the Albigeois, the oldest of four boys, and was raised in Toulouse, where his father Jean de Coras, a licentiate in law, was an advocate in the Parlement. Already at the age of thirteen,

young Jean was interpreting the civil law from a podium in
Toulouse (or so the story goes), and in his next years, while
studying civil and canon law at Angers, Orléans, and Paris,
he was often asked to teach as well. He then went to Padua,
offered one hundred propositions as subjects for his doctoral
dissertation, and won acclaim for his felicitous responses. In
1536 at the age of twenty-one, he was granted his doctorate
by Philippus Decius, "that great luminary of the law."
(Coras said later that Decius was then so senile he could not
remember a word of the law, and spent fifteen minutes trying to utter the first phrase of his oration. Finally the degree
had to be granted by someone else. The anecdote suggests
that Coras did not always take himself so seriously as a
young prodigy.)

Returning to Toulouse, Coras was hired as a regent at the
university and became celebrated as a lecturer on the civil
law. He himself reports the applause of his listeners, while
Usilis says that no one could remember any professor drawing such crowds. He personally had been present when
Coras had poured forth his spellbinding oratory before two
thousand people, "his voice smooth, flowing, clear, and me-
lodious." This is all the more impressive when we realize
that law lectures at Toulouse were often given from five to
ten o'clock in the morning.[3]

During those years of early glory, Coras had another relation with the law, not mentioned by Usilis: he became a liti-
gant. His mother Jeanne de Termes died at Réalmont and
by her testament of 1542 left him all her goods and property. Master Jean Coras the elder obstructed the execution
of the will, and Master Jean de Coras the younger sued him
in a case finally decided in 1544 by the Parlement of Toulouse. The son's inheritance was confirmed and the father
ordered to allow him to make an inventory, but Coras senior was given usufruct of the goods and property for the

rest of his life. The two men made up eventually—Coras was to dedicate a work to him in 1549—but like the comic presentation of his doctoral ceremony, the suit against his father suggests some ambivalence in his attitudes toward order and authority.[4]

Meanwhile Coras himself became a husband and father, and much to his delight. "Fortunate matrimony" he said in his legal text *De Ritu Nuptiarum*, and he inserted a section on his wife Catherine Boysonné, the daughter of a Toulouse merchant, right into his commentary. The couple soon had children, a daughter Jeanne and then a son Jacques, the latter also warranting a notice in the midst of a legal discussion. "Yesterday April 13, 1546, I was moved with incredible joy, for I became through our healthy Catherine the father of a little son."[5]

Sought after as teacher, Coras moved his family to Valence, where he gave instruction in civil law from 1545 through 1549, and then spent two years lecturing at Ferrara. All this time he was writing and publishing Latin commentaries on the Roman law, on subjects ranging from marriage and contracts to judicial actions and the constitution of the state. At least from 1541 on, he had been sending his manuscripts to printing houses, especially in Lyon, the center for legal publications. And the law students loved his books. "Corasissima" one of them wrote in the margin next to an especially apt phrase on the subject of inheritance by minors.

The editions also reveal two interesting sides to Coras. First, a willingness to grow, to rethink, to reinterpret. He often tells his readers, "I first worked on this in Toulouse in such and such a year, I am revising it now in Ferrara." Second, a shrewd sense of how to advance his career. His earliest books are already dedicated to the First President of the Parlement of Paris and to Mansencal, First President of the

Parlement of Toulouse. The cardinals of Châtillon and Lorraine are sent appropriate works when the time comes.[6]

This paid off in January 1553, when a vacancy occurred in the Parlement of Toulouse. He had returned to that city from Ferrara for a sad reason: his wife Catherine Boysonné died and he came back for a period of mourning. Henri II profited by his presence in France to seek advice on royal dealings with the duke and the cardinal of Ferrara, and then appointed Coras to the opening. In February 1553, Jean de Coras took his oath as judge, or *conseiller*, in the Parlement where his father had long been an advocate.[7]

In the seven years that passed between Coras's new judicial role and the case of Martin Guerre, his life took other new turnings. He married again; he became more and more interested in the Protestant cause; and he began to think of other goals for his publications. His second wife was Jacquette de Bussi, a widow and his cousin, and also the niece of a royal Master of Requests. Childless from her first marriage, she remained so in her second, but mothered Jacques de Coras sufficiently to refer to him always as "my son." We know of Jean's relations with her mostly from letters exchanged several years after the trial, but they can nonetheless suggest his own experience of marriage in the earlier period.[8]

Coras is expressively, deeply, almost foolishly fond of Jacquette de Bussi. "Never wife present or absent was so cherished and loved by husband as you are and will be." "I beg you believe that day and night at every hour and minute I dream of you, I wait for you, I desire you and love you so much that without you I don't exist." He sends her books to read, "a naughty dress," and "two pens well formed and split to my taste like you," and tells her if it is cold at Réalmont, "don't sleep alone, so long as it's not with a monk" (a pun—*moine* was an old French word for "bedwarmer"). He gives her political reports and news of the Reformed cause; he instructs her about how to receive important visitors and messages to deliver. He frets about her health and about whether she returns his affection. When he does not hear from her, he writes, "this makes me believe in spite of myself that I am not so engraved in the bowels of your memory as I have always wished."

In fact, Jacquette is somewhat reserved toward her husband. The game of their marriage is that he is the pursuer and she the pursued. He signs his letters "Your your your and a hundred thousand times your Jean de Coras"; she signs hers "Your very humble and obedient wife." He earnestly seeks her opinion on whether he should accept an important post; she writes back "your will be done," which brings from him a wounded letter with a formal signature, as on a decree. Meanwhile, despite ill health, she runs their properties with great competence, renting out lands, having fences repaired, reviewing taille books, and ordering fields to be sown with millet and oats. She sends him news and books she has read, garters she has stitched for him, capons and medicinal water for his eyes. She hopes he is "content and joyous."[9]

Husband and wife were especially united by their commitment to the new religion. For Jean de Coras, there were many channels by which he could have learned about Protestantism—for example, from people around the Duchess Renée in Ferrara, that center for religious refugees from France. When his major text on canon law appeared in 1548, the *Paraphrasis in universam sacerdotiorum materiam*, he certainly was not yet a convert: he accepts the legitimacy of the papacy, saying merely that the pope should always be a faithful pastor and not a tyrant. By 1557, his treatise against clandestine marriages is at least consistent with Protestant sentiments in its critique of canon law, its anticipation that he would be attacked by "venomous calumny . . . under pretext of religion," and its affirmation that all its arguments "conformed to the word of God."[10]

Coras's *Petit discours . . . Des mariages clandestinement et irreveremment contractes* marked another departure in his life. It was the first book he published in the vernacular. The goal of this Gascon was not the usual literary one of enriching the French language, "for which I confess to be little favored by my native and thorny way of speaking." Rather he wanted to influence public opinion: parental consent to their children's marriages was a subject that "belonged no less to those without knowledge of letters than to the trained, learned, and scholarly." He dedicated the book to Henri II, whose recent edict on clandestine marriages he was here supporting and who not long afterward granted to Coras a nine-year "privilege," a monopoly on sales, for any work of his own that he wanted to publish or reprint. This unusual gift permitted Coras more control than most authors of his day over the printing of and profits from his writing. He used it in 1558 for a French translation of a dialogue between the emperor Hadrian and the philosopher Epictetus, dedicated to the Dauphin, and then in 1560 for his great synthetic work on the structure of law, *De iuris Arte*, dedicated to the Chancellor of France.[11]

···•———◀◆▶———•···

In 1560, when Jean de Coras took up his tasks in the Criminal Chamber, he was forty-five years old and, as the above evidence suggests, he was not a man of uniform sentiments and consistent goals. He had shaped a brilliant career but he also had made a higher commitment to Protestantism, which would eventually cost him career and life. As a spe-

IEAN·DE·CORAS·   CE·DE·A·raifon

IEAN DE CORAS IE IVris confulte Con.er au Parlement de Thoulouse
Et Chancelier de Navarre·
   TON Eloquent Scauoir et ta Rare Vertu·
   Remplirent de leur bruit la France et L'Italie
   Et Malgre' Les Rigueurs, dont tu Fus Combatu
   Tu Souhus en Mourant la Gloire de ta Uie
      Bastet · excudit ·

Jean de Coras in the late 1560s, a seventeenth-century copy
by Bastet of a lost original

cialist in the Roman law, he was a firm believer in the ordered family and in the power of the sovereign ("subjects
must obey their magistrates like their own parents,"he
said), but he was soon to be implicated in Protestant resis-
tance movements in Toulouse and in France. He warns families against "the reckless passions of love," but at the very
thought that he can collect his wife a month hence, he runs
to get out the trunk and begins packing her taffeta skirts.[12]

When Jean de Coras came into contact with "Martin
Guerre," he recognized a man with some of his own qualities. Peasant though he was, the prisoner was poised, intel-
ligent, and (especially) eloquent. "He seemed not merely to
be recounting things to the judges," said Le Sueur, "but to
make them come to life before their eyes." "I do not remember having read of any man who had so successful a
memory," said Coras.[13] He also seemed an honorable family
man, in love with his beautiful wife. That he had sued his
uncle for the accounts did not seem so outrageous to a son
who had sued his father for an inventory. If I am right that
"Martin Guerre" was a Protestant sympathizer, Coras
would have had yet another reason to find him a person he
could believe.

Then the man with the wooden leg appeared in court
"like a miracle," an act of providence, of God's grace, to
protect Pierre Guerre and to show Jean de Coras that he was
wrong.[14] Coras had been thinking about the dangers of
lying a couple of years earlier in his translation of the dialogue between Hadrian and Epictetus.

> Hadrian: What is it that man can not see?
> Epictetus: The heart and the thought of others.

The judge comments, "And in truth there is nothing between men more detestable than feigning and dissimulat-

ing, though our century is so unfortunate that in every estate, he who knows best how to refine his lies, his pretenses and his hypocrisy is often the most revered."[15]

Did Coras ever dream that he would be so fooled, and by someone whose tricks he had to admire? What a well-wrought and longlasting achievement was this imposture—"the thousand necessary lies" of Arnaud du Tilh. ("He answered so well," said Le Sueur, "he almost seemed to be playing.") Lawyers, royal officers, and would-be courtiers knew all about self-fashioning—to use Stephen Greenblatt's term— about the molding of speech, manners, gesture, and conversation that had helped them to advance, as did any newcomer to high position in the sixteenth century. Where does self-fashioning stop and lying begin? Long before Montaigne posed that question to his readers in a self-accusatory essay, Pansette's inventiveness posed it to his judges.[16]

Coras's first response was to deny that this was a case of human inventiveness. Instead, Arnaud was a magician, aided by an evil spirit. He was a treacherous person and Coras could have no regrets about his death, neither from a judicial nor from a moral point of view. Coras's second response was to recognize that there was something deeply fascinating about Arnaud du Tilh which spoke to his own conflicting feelings and to the situation of the people in his own class—and that there was something not only profoundly wrong but also profoundly right about the invented marriage of the new Martin and Bertrande de Rols.

So he sat down at his desk and sharpened his pens. Another new turn in his work, another edition in French. But most of all this book would allow him to judge once again the man he had just executed: to condemn him once again, but also to give him, or at least his story, another chance.

II

Histoire prodigieuse, Histoire tragique

C ORAS'S *Arrest Memorable* is an innovative book of con-
tradictory images and mixed genres. Le Sueur's *Admiranda historia*, though it has some original features to it,
fits readily into the genre of the news account, so important
in this century before the periodical press. A pamphlet of
small format, it simply tells the story from the arrival of the
Guerres in Artigat to the execution of Arnaud du Tilh,
drawing an appropriate moral at the end. "A friend" in
Toulouse sent the manuscript to Jean de Tournes, the celebrated humanist printer of Lyon, who sometimes published
news accounts. He did not even wait to get a royal privilege
for the work, but printed it in Latin right away. Another
copy came into the hands of the publisher Vincent Sertenas
in Paris. By the end of January 1561, Sertenas had had the
work translated into French and had acquired a six-year
privilege for it from the king. He published it without the
name of its author, under the title *Histoire Admirable d'un
Faux et Supposé Mary, advenue en Languedoc, l'an mil cinq cens
soixante*. News of the imposture began to circulate like
other "terrible" and "marvelous" cases of murder, adultery,
fire, and flood.[1]

Meanwhile on February 2, 1561, Jean de Coras signed the

dedication of his manuscript and sent it to the merchant-publisher Antoine Vincent of Lyon, transferring to him his rights under the general nine-year privilege. Until that year Vincent had brought out very few books in the vernacular; rather he had built his fortune on Latin editions, including Coras's *De actionibus* of 1555 and his *De iuris Arte* of 1560.[2] The new title had much that was alluring and fresh about it to a buyer of 1561: *Arrest Memorable, du Parlement du Tolose, Contenant une histoire prodigieuse, de nostre temps, avec cent belles, & doctes Annotations, de monsieur maistre Jean de Coras, Conseiller en ladite cour, & rapporteur du proces. Prononcé es Arrestz Generaulx le xii Septembre MDLX.*

Judgments in criminal cases were sometimes published in France, such as that of the Italian condemned for having poisoned the Dauphin of France in 1536. Collections of decrees, civil and criminal, were beginning to appear.[3] But here the sentence took up only two pages of a 117-page book, and the judge himself, rather than reserving his comments for a learned treatise on criminal law, was broadcasting them far and wide. Coras may be the first legal figure in France to exploit one of his own criminal cases for a work in the vernacular.*

And then there was that phrase, "a prodigious history." Very much in the air these days were collections of "prodigies"—of wondrous plants and animals, of double suns and

---

*Since the Edict of Villars-Cotteret in 1539, all judicial procedure had to be in French. In civil cases, which were open to the public, the lawyers' formal pleas were sometimes printed and became by the end of the sixteenth century an appreciated literary genre (Catherine E. Holmes, *L'Eloquence judiciaire de 1620 à 1660* [Paris, 1967]). Criminal cases, in contrast, were in principle closed to the public until the reading of the sentence, and, as in the Martin Guerre case, there might often be no pleading by lawyers. This meant that any subsequent literary treatment of the case required much reconstruction by the author.

monstrous births. Just the year before Vincent Sertenas had brought out the *Histoires prodigieuses* of Pierre Boaistuau, and when he published Le Sueur's little book, the term was transferred in an opening sonnet to the story of the false Martin: "The most prodigious stories you can read/From Christian times or pagan . . ./Will seem like nothing to you/After the sham husband." Coras put the word right in his title, using it with the same meaning as Boaistuau, who had once been his student at Valence. The prodigious is strange, though not necessarily unique; it is more rare than other events of its kind. So this imposture surpassed any others that had been heard of.[4]

The inside of Coras's book at first glance resembles a traditional legal commentary, with its dialectic between Text and Annotation. In fact most of the Text is not an official document that Coras is citing, but rather what he calls "Texte de la toile du procès,"[5] the web of the case, spun by Coras himself; and the Annotations often have nothing to do with the law.

This new use of a traditional form gave more freedom to Coras than he had enjoyed before, even though his Latin treatises had been quite wide-ranging. First it gave him a chance to comment on central issues in the legal practice of his day: witnesses, evidence, torture, and the nature of proof. Here was a case where the "best" witnesses turned out to be mistaken, hearsay evidence turned out to be true, and the judges almost went astray. It gave him a chance to discuss marriage and its problems, the wedding of children before the age of puberty, impotence, desertion, and adultery.[6] There was also room for religious reflection on such matters as blasphemy and for some sly digs at Catholicism. Holy wafers and special cakes as a means to lift a spell of impotence were "vain superstitions"; one should pray and fast instead. His annotation on magic also reveals a Protestant sensibility: redeemed by Christ's passion, we must beg him to "raise our hearts ... so that by the light of his words, we can chase away all the illusions, artifices, and impostures, by which the devil always tries to trap the children of God and his Church."[7]

Was there any more fundamental sense in which Coras saw the story of Martin Guerre as conveying a Protestant message? Some of the circumstances surrounding its appearance suggest that there was. The publisher Antoine Vincent was a major figure in the French Reformed Church; later in 1561, he acquired the royal privilege for the Calvinist Psalter, a vernacular bestseller that was to outstrip the *Arrest Memorable*. Coras dedicated the book to Jean de Monluc, bishop of Valence, whose ideas were found heretical by the Paris Theology Faculty that same year. Le Sueur's initial publication also had something of a Protestant setting: an author moving toward Calvinist sentiments; a dedication to Judge Michel Du Faur, suspected of heretical sympathies; a printer, Jean de Tournes, who was a supporter of the new religion. Could the woes of the Guerres ever have come about, Coras and Le Sueur may have asked, in the Reformed city of Geneva, where a new law and an assiduous Consistory would never have permitted so youthful a marriage, would have divorced Bertrande betimes, and would have quickly uncovered adultery? And was it not a Protestant God sending back the man with the wooden leg in time to undo the overweening confidence of the judges of the Parlement of Toulouse?[8]

If Coras and Le Sueur had such views, it must be said that they are not imposed by their texts. The *Arrest Memorable* easily found readers of both religions, and it was printed later in Paris by Catholic houses. Vincent Sertenas, Le

Sueur's publisher in Paris, was also Catholic. Coras's dedication suggests only the light purposes of the book: it had "an argument so beautiful, so delectable, and so monstrously strange" that it should bring the bishop recreation and release from his worries.[9]

Indeed, mixture in tone and mixture in form are the central characteristics of the *Arrest Memorable*. Here is a law book that calls into question the workings of the law; an historical account that raises doubts about its own truth. This is a text that moves among the moral tale, comedy, and tragedy. Heroes seem villains and villains seem heroes, and the story is told in two ways at the same time.

The legal matrix of the *Arrest Memorable* helps to create this complexity. The Text is organized like Coras's report to the Chamber, where he had to develop arguments both for and against the accused. Now he can set off a Text in which he refers to "the defendant" and "the said du Tilh" against Annotations in which he refers to "this rustic," "this lewd fellow," and "this prodigious offender."

In addition, Coras exaggerates certain things and omits others—we might even say that he lies a little—in shaping his account. First, he makes Arnaud du Tilh's memory even more marvelous than it was: Le Sueur reports at least his forgetting the name of a godparent at Martin Guerre's confirmation, but in Coras he never forgets. Second, he presents himself and the court as less convinced of Arnaud's innocence than in fact they were. He never mentions that Bertrande and Pierre were imprisoned for months, a fact given by Le Sueur and, more important, recorded twice in the registers of the Parlement. The sentence of September 12, 1560, actually describes Bertrande de Rols and Pierre Guerre as "formerly prisoners in connection with the matter"; as he reproduces the decree in his book, Coras supresses all of this and substitutes "etc."

Nor was the omission simply to save space, for Coras added to the printed decree several crimes of which Arnaud du Tilh was not actually convicted : "abduction, sacrilege, plagiat [in Roman law, stealing a person for sale or other abuse], larceny, and other actions committed by the said prisoner."[10] Coras's annotation on these crimes made them essentially extensions of fraudulent impersonation and adultery, but they also gave him a chance to argue that Bertrande was coerced and that the death penalty was warranted.*

On the whole these exaggerations and omisssions worked to strengthen the *Arrest Memorable* as a moral tale. Arnaud du Tilh's prodigious qualities are built up by comparison with biblical, classical, and more recent impostors. The physical resemblance that nature allowed between unrelated people was already strange enough but, search as he might, Coras could find no example where resemblance both of face and of manner—the "thousand necessary lies"—had been so successful for so long. In the thirteenth century, the false Count Baldwin of Flanders, despite his many proofs, had always been doubted by the count's daughter Jeanne. Here the relatives had accepted the impostor and, "what must arouse greater admiration," even his own wife had lived with him familiarly for over three years "without ever perceiving or even suspecting the fraud." This version of the case assigns the full dazzling power of deception to Arnaud. It permits the accusation that he is a magician—Coras says he could not rid himself of this opinion even though du Tilh denied any diabolic art—and it leads without doubt to du Tilh's exemplary execution. It also casts Bertrande as a

---

*Coras had difficulty only with larceny, for Justinian had not prescribed death for this crime. By showing that the theft was large (Martin's inheritance) and that it involved treachery and disturbing the peace of marriage, Coras said it could warrant punishment by death (pp. 126–127).

dupe, understandable given "the weakness of her sex, easily deceived by the cunning and craftiness of men."[11]

But there is something bothersome about this version, to husbands and lovers both. In those frequent comic stories of the time, where one person is substituted for another for lovemaking in the dark of night, it is rare that the tricked person can tell the difference. (I know of only one counterexample: the old knight in the *Cent Nouvelles Nouvelles*, who notes the difference between the serving maid's firm breasts and his wife's mature form.[12]) But Bertrande's was a true story, not a titillating literary convention, and it went on for more than a night. Was the weakness of the sex really so great that wives could not tell the difference between married love and adultery? The cuckolded Martin Guerre clearly thought not, as we know from the words attributed to him in court by both Coras and Le Sueur. And it is hard to imagine that the Coras we have seen dealing with Jacquette de Bussi could consistently believe that women were so easy to trick.*

The judge left other loopholes in his moral tale which allowed it to be recast in another genre. Where is its hero? A moral tale is supposed to begin with the hero's departure, and end with his return, his unseating of the false hero, and his marriage. But Martin Guerre's departure is for the most part reproved; his return, though providential, shows him unforgiving and unrepentant; he does not win the memory contest with Pansette; and Coras gives no indication that the subsequent reunion with Bertrande will be a happy one.

---

*His dealings with his daughter Jeanne de Coras also suggest he held her in high regard. In September 1559 he translated *Les Douze reigles* of Giovanni Pico della Mirandola from Latin into French for her, to serve as a defense in time of temptation. The work appeared in print in 1565 in Lyon, along with a new edition of the *Arrest Memorable*.

Le Sueur, who also treats Martin with little sympathy, at least included the scene in which President Mansencal tried to reconcile Martin and Bertrande; this is missing from Coras.[13]

An even more curious omission from the first edition of the *Arrest Memorable* is the account of Arnaud du Tilh's confession and execution. That there was a confession is mentioned twice in passing[14]—a hurried reader might not digest the fact—but the 1561 edition breaks off when the condemned man is sent to the judge of Rieux. Coras leaves his audience some room for doubt about whether the Criminal Chamber actually did get the right man.

Only in the 1565 edition does Coras eliminate ambiguity by describing what Arnaud confessed at Artigat, and the ambiguity is reintroduced immediately by a new Annotation in which he describes the whole story as a "tragedy":

> Text: Seeing and considering that the most private and particular friends of the said Martin Guerre mistook him for Martin . . . he got the idea to play the tragedy you have been hearing. Annotation CIIII: It was truly a tragedy for this fine peasant, all the more because the outcome was wretched, indeed fatal for him. Or at least it makes it hard to tell the difference between tragedy and comedy.

The printer of the 1572 edition elaborated on this, using the word "tragicomedy," which was increasingly finding its way into sixteenth-century French literary theory and practice.* "The Protasis, or opening, is joyous, pleasant and diverting, containing the ruses and cunning tricks of a false and supposed husband." (Readers might think they were holding

---

*Interestingly enough, the term "tragicomedy" is first used in the prologue to Plautus' *Amphitryon*, a play about impostures, which had editions in Latin and French in the early sixteenth century.

in their hands Boccaccio's *Decameron* or the *Heptameron* of
Marguerite of Navarre or the picaresque *Lazarillo de
Tormes*.) "The Epitasis, or middle part, uncertain and
doubtful because of the disputes and contention during the
trial. The Catastrophe or issue of the Morality is sad, pitiful
and miserable." Le Sueur, too, put his simpler account in
another light by calling it a tragedy several times.[15]

The originality of Coras's vision of this peasant story
should be stressed. The French tragicomedy ended happily
and used aristocratic figures for its leading personages. The
Histoires tragiques of the Italian Bandello, translated, retold,
and published by Pierre Boaistuau in 1559, did connect the
tragic with "prodigious" passion—an association also suggested by Arnaud and Bertrande—but none of the characters
there were villagers. That Coras could conceive of "a play of
tragedy between persons of low estate" depended on his
being able to identify himself somewhat with the rustic
who had remade himself.[16]

In Coras's "comitragic" version, Arnaud du Tilh still has
certain prodigious qualities. He is compared to Jupiter dis-
guised as Amphitryon in order to seduce his wife. He is
compared with and found to surpass the great rememberers
of antiquity, such as Seneca's friend Portius Latro. But he
also has accomplices, including Bertrande who, not at all
deceived, decides to fashion a marriage with him. (This
Bertrande is present in Coras's text, but is less prominent
than the duped wife. The possibility of an honorable woman
disposing of her body as she pleases is much more disturbing than the self-fashioning of Pansette. It is the subject of
nightmares, as when Coras writes to Jacquette of "a strange
dream that I had yesterday that before my eyes you were remarried to another, and when I reproached you for the
wrong you were doing me, you responded by turning your

back on me."[17]) Here one can approve the cuckolding of the once impotent and now faraway husband. Here Arnaud du Tilh becomes a kind of hero, a more real Martin Guerre than the hard-hearted man with the wooden leg. The tragedy is more in his unmasking than in his imposture.

12
Of the Lame

⋯•──◀━◆━▶──•⋯

"I'M SENDING YOU ... one of my *Arrests* of Martin Guerre, newly reprinted for the fifth time," Jean de Coras wrote his wife in December 1567. He could take pride in how well his book was doing, even perhaps in the editions published in Paris and Brussels in 1565 in violation of his nine-year privilege. The format was smaller now, a sure sign that the book cost less and that publishers were expecting to reach a larger market. In early 1572 Parisian publishers brought it out under their own royal grant for ten years.[1]

By then Coras was rarely thinking about the *Arrest Memorable*. He had quarreled first with his Catholic colleagues in the Parlement after the Calvinist uprising in Toulouse in May 1562 (witnesses claimed that arquebuses were fired from the windows of Coras's townhouse, which he hotly denied). By early 1568 the Protestant judges had not only been expelled from the Parlement but were condemned for high treason and hanged in effigy. Coras was serving the cause as chancellor for the Huguenot queen of Navarre, Jeanne d'Albret. Back in Toulouse after peace was made, he and François de Ferrières were imprisoned in the wake of the Saint Bartholomew's Day massacres in Paris. In October

1572 they were lynched in their red robes by a Catholic mob in front of the Parlement building.[2]

Coras's works continued to be published, however. While people were fighting about the true and false church and the devil's deceptions, the book about the impostor-husband had another Paris printing in 1579. Latin translations of the first edition came out in Frankfurt in 1576 and 1588 (one of them finding its way to England) and then at the end of the century in Lyon, publisher Barthélemy Vincent took up his father's author once again.[3]

The book was bought first and foremost by lawyers and judges, who signed their names in the flyleaves, wrote notes in the margins, had it bound together with Coras's *Paraphraze sur l'Edict des Mariages clandestinement contractez* or with other books on marriage law. By the early seventeenth century, "l'arrest de Martin Guerre" was listed among central texts for anyone being trained in jurisprudence. But it was also being enjoyed for wider literary purposes; one such reader bound it together with Le Sueur's *Admiranda historia*.[4]

Le Sueur's work followed the expected path of a news account as it is printed and reprinted and transformed into a popular legend. In the first edition in French, Le Sueur's comparisons with Jupiter, Mercury, Amphitryon, and Sosius had disappeared; Artigat had become "Artigne" and du Tilh "Tylie," never again to be corrected. By the time of a 1615 edition, Bertrande has become "a woman of note" in the title and the event has become timeless—taking place "during these last troubles"—with no reference to the battle of Saint-Quentin and Philip II.[5]

We know something of the reaction to the story from those readers who decided to retell it or comment on it. Jean Papon, royal judge in the Forez, included it in his *Re-*

cueil d'arrestz notables of 1565 under the section on adultery. He was especially struck by the "multiplication of crimes" of Arnaud du Tilh (a multiplication, we recall, performed by Coras for the printed edition) and considered that almost anyone of them might deserve the death penalty. For Géraud de Maynard, a former student of Coras and later judge in the Parlement of Toulouse, it was Bernarde du Tilh's legitimacy and her right to inherit the goods of her condemned father which made up the *Notables . . . Questions du Droit.* Etienne Pasquier featured the case of Martin Guerre in his *Recherches de la France* among other trials that had ended with miraculous proofs. Drawing details especially from Le Sueur's account, the distinguished Paris judge thought—and he was sure women would agree—that Martin Guerre ought to have been punished for having abandoned his wife in the first place.[6]

For those writers less interested in the points of law, it was the marvelous, the "prodigious" features of the story that were appealing. The scholar-printer Henri Estienne used it to show that a story from Herodotus of successful imposture was not so unbelievable. Gilbert Cousin and Antoine Du Verdier sandwiched it in between accounts of peasant revolts, comets and floods, transformations of females into males, and political conspiracies. François de Belleforest placed it in a chapter on remarkable physical resemblances in his continuation of Boaistuau's *Histoires prodigieuses.* (He was evidently in the crowd the day the sentence was pronounced at Toulouse. One wonders if Belleforest recalled that Pansette was his fellow countryman when he said that the husbands of the Comminges treat their wives "gently and not with that roughness that is imputed to Gascons."[7])

Whatever their literary or professional motives, all these

DE DEVX GENTILS-
hommes se rapportans tellement de face, voix, parole & gestes qu'il estoit impossible de les discerner en sorte quelconque.

Histoire premiere.

IE n'ignore point qu'entre les grands miracles de la nature on n'aie de tout

A case of remarkable resemblance in the sixteenth century, from François de Belleforest, *Histoires prodigieuses* (Paris, 1574)

writers were in accord in making Arnaud du Tilh the inventive figure in the tale, to be admired and feared, envied and rejected. Some mentioned the possibility of magic but did not stress it, since impersonation was not the kind of damage that witches were being accused of in contemporary trials.[8] The self-fashioning Bertrande has entirely disappeared from these retellings, as have any doubts about the rightness of the sentence. It should be added, however, that we have no female commentary on the story until the twentieth century. Jacquette de Bussi's reaction to her husband's gift book is unrecorded. I doubt that she believed that Bertrande de Rols could have been deceived for so long.*

There are two exceptions to these generalizations about male responses to the story of Martin Guerre. One comes from the poet Auger Gaillard, Protestant and former soldier from the Albigeois. In his *Amours prodigieuses* of 1592, published in French and Occitan, he identifies not with the "hardened deceiver" ("le trompeur aguerri") but with the tricked wife:

> . . . in Béarn and in France
> Many girls have I seen with the same appearance,
> So they could change places readily
> And deceive me easily.

He rejoices that he is in love with a Moorish woman, whom he would be able to recognize even if he had been absent a hundred years.[9]

The other exception is Montaigne in his "Des boyteux"

---

*The charming novel by Janet Lewis, *The Wife of Martin Guerre*, differs from my historical account in most respects, but they resemble each other in presenting a Bertrande who is not a dupe and who has some independence of spirit.

(Of the Lame), which first appeared in 1588.[10] It is often thought that this essay introduces the Toulouse case only incidentally to a discussion of why witches should not be burned, but in fact the issues that Montaigne raises are not confined to sorcery and there are echoes of Coras and his text throughout. Montaigne insists how difficult it is to know the truth about things and how uncertain an instrument is human reason. "Truth and falsehood have both alike countenances ... Wee beholde them with one same eye." Montaigne himself admits to getting carried away in the heat of an argument, exaggerating the naked truth by the vigor of his words. Yet we all insist upon our opinions, forcing them on others by iron and fire. Better to be tentative than to be recklessly sure, to be an apprentice at sixty than to present oneself as a doctor at ten.

It is at this point, at the very center of "Des boyteux," that Montaigne talks explicitly of the case of Martin Guerre:

> Being yong, I saw a law case, which Corras, a Counsellor of Tholouse, caused to be printed, of a strange accident of two men, who presented themselves one for another. I remember (and I remember nothing else so well) that me thought he proved his imposture, whom he condemned as guiltie, so wondrous-strange and so far-exceeding both our knowledge and his owne, who was judge, that I found much boldness in the sentence, which had condemned him to be hanged.

Montaigne would have withheld his judgment, like the sixty peasants of Artigat and Sajas who could not tell the difference between Martin Guerre and Arnaud du Tilh.*

---

*It should be remembered that at the end of the trial, which Montaigne witnessed, Arnaud du Tilh was still maintaining that he was Martin Guerre. Moreover, Montaigne may have read only the first edition of Coras's *Arrest*, which does not spell out Arnaud's confession.

Let us receive some forme of sentence that may say: "The Court understands nothing of it," more freely and ingenuously than did the Areopagites, who finding themselves urged and entangled in a case they could not well cleare or determine, appointed the parties to come againe and appeare before them a hundred yeares after.

Montaigne stresses the poor evidence there is for such irrevocable decisions as burning a witch. To kill people, one needs a luminous and sharp clarity. He cites the Italian proverb that "He knowes not the perfect pleasure of Venus that hath not layne with a limping woman." Some people apply it to men as well, arguing that what they lack in their legs they make up for in their genitals. Is not this a supreme example of the lameness of our reasoning, of how our imagination gets the best of us? Montaigne wonders about the "termeritie" of those who judge; for him "there is no other sentence or arrest than that of necessitie, and impuissance to proceede further."

Montaigne is too hard on the long-dead Coras in "Des boyteux," but in a curious way his essay expresses an essential message of the *Arrest Memorable*. Coras had acted like a doctor when he was little more than ten, and the device with which he signed his book was "A raison cède" (To reason yield); yet he had admitted at forty-five how his reason had misled him and how difficult it was for a judge to separate truth from lies. Coras had recommended a death sentence when he might have recommended the galleys or banishment, but it was his own multivalent representation of the case that made it possible for Montaigne to rebuke him. And Montaigne's task was easier: he was writing not as a judge but "by way of discourse," whereas Coras had faced a divided family and village awaiting the court's decision.

Reading the *Arrest Memorable* and Montaigne's essay to-

Punishment arrives on a wooden leg, from Otto Vaenius,
Quinti Horatii Flacci Emblemata (Antwerp, 1612)

gether gives each a new meaning. Montaigne keeps coming back to images of legs: the gouty legs of the prince supposedly cured by the "wondrous deedes" of a priest; the thin legs of the French and the thick legs of Germanicus, both explained by horseback riding; the deformed legs of the pleasure-giving lame woman. He himself is deformed, that is, difficult to understand:"I have seene no such monster, or more expresse wonder in this world than myself ... The more I frequent and know myselfe, the more my deformitie astonieth me and the lesse I understand myselfe." The legs of Martin Guerre and Arnaud du Tilh had also been a source of controversy, but was even the man "arrived from Spain with a wooden leg" all that clear a sign? From Horace, one knew that punishment comes on a limping leg, but nonetheless catches up to even the fleetest criminal. But one also knew the popular saying that lies come on a limping leg, for you can't go very far with them.[11] Coras believed he had found out who the impostor was, but at the heart of his *Arrest Memorable* is an uncertainty as unsettling as Montaigne's.

Epilogue

····—◆►—····

IN 1563, when our next information is available about the
village of Artigat, everyone is back in place and doubts
are gradually being plowed under. Pierre Guerre and Martin
Guerre are brought to settle a dispute among two neighboring families; it is decided that A. Rols will be one of
those to arbitrate the quarrel and everyone agrees to stick by
the decision. Pierre still has dealings with the court of
Rieux, however; he has sued an important rural merchant,
James Delhure, and his wife Bernarde. This may well have
been an effort to regain for the Guerre family some of the
property sold by Arnaud du Tilh. Coras had thought that
Martin Guerre would have a right to void these contracts,
though the buyers should be allowed to keep whatever profits they had made from the land in the interim.[1]

About Martin Guerre and Bertrande de Rols there is no
immediate evidence, but we can see that there was a basis
for an armistice between them. If she were an adulterer,
then he was a cuckold. (In any case, there was an old local
tradition that reconciled adulterers to their spouses with the
payment of a fine.[2]) She had to live down her easy acceptance of the impostor, he his irresponsible desertion of the
family. He now had wondrous adventures to recount of his

life with the great in faraway places, and he needed a wife to
take care of him in his infirmity. (The popular terror of
being crippled is suggestd by the Languedoc curse "le mau-
lubec vous trousse," may your leg-sores turn you lame.[3])
She now had all kinds of skills and an authority she had
lacked before, and she needed a husband and father for her
children.* Someone may have had to give way on the question of religion, for Martin probably returned from his cardinal and his house of Saint John of Jerusalem a good Catholic, while Bertrande may have been a Protestant.

Even Bertrande's marriage bed had new activity in it, so
one learns from the division of properties made among the
sons of the late Martin Guerre in 1594. Sanxi had died, but
not before passing on his name to a godson in the next
generation, Sanxi Rols. The tileworks, three houses, and numerous parcels of land on either side of the Lèze are split
among Pierre and Gaspard Guerre, Martin's sons by Bertrande, and Pierre the younger, his son (born around 1575)
by his second wife.[4] (Martin's descendants are clearly living
in Languedoc rather than Basque fashion.) In the mid-sev-
enteenth century there is again a Martin Guerre in the village, and he has at least six other relatives carrying on the
family name, including Master Dominique the notary;
Anne de Guerre is well married to a Banquels. The Guerres
and the Rols are on the best of terms, serving as godparents
to each other's children, owning neighboring properties,
and in some cases holding fields jointly.[5]

Does this mean that life went on as if the imposture had
never occurred? that the values of rightful succession and
contracted marriage rolled along and obliterated all trace of

---

*Bernarde du Tilh evidently stayed with her mother. Arnaud du Tilh's
goods had been adjudged to her "in order that Martin not be responsible for
giving her a dowry." Le Sueur, *Histoire*, E ii^r.

invention? I think not. Bertrande could not have forgotten her life with Arnaud du Tilh, and the village must have found a way to talk about it without rekindling old disputes too much. That word reached them about Coras's book seems certain—surely the notaries and merchants going back and forth to Rieux would hear of it—but it also seems very unlikely that the Artigatois would want the *Arrest Memorable* read aloud at their evening gatherings or would accept this outsider's version as their own. The local story would be told along with other news of the latest village bastard or the latest migrant from the Lèze valley to Spain, who took a concubine and had a second family during his years there.[6] But it lasted, beyond the other anecdotes and through major upheavals such as the Wars of Religion.

Some twenty-eight years ago in Artigat, a young mother, herself a recent immigrant from French Catalonia, was complaining over her baby carriage to a village grandmother, "Nothing ever happens in Artigat." "Perhaps not now," answered the grandmother, "but in the sixteenth century . . . " And she related the story of Martin Guerre.

The story of Martin Guerre is told and retold because it reminds us that astonishing things are possible. Even for the historian who has deciphered it, it retains a stubborn vitality. I think I have uncovered the true face of the past—or has Pansette done it once again?

Selected Bibliography of Writings on Martin Guerre

Entries are organized chronologically by the date of the first edition. Subsequent editions and translations are indicated under the first edition.

Jean de Coras, *Arrest Memorable, du Parlement de Tolose, Contenant une histoire prodigieuse, de nostre temps, avec cent belles, & doctes Annotations, de monsieur maistre Jean de Coras, Conseiller en ladite Cour, & rapporteur du proces. Prononcé es Arrestz Generaulx le xii Septembre MDLX.* Lyon: Antoine Vincent, 1561. Avec Privilege du Roy. (Quarto.)

> Reprinted in Paris, 1565, in octavo, without privilege and without the name of the printer.
> Reprinted in Bruges: Hubert Goltz, 1565.

———*Arrest Memorable . . . avec cent et onze belles, et doctes annotations . . . Item, Les Douze Reigles du Seigneur Iean Pic de la Mirandole . . . traduites de Latin en François par ledit de Coras.* Lyon: Antoine Vincent, 1565. Avec privilege du Roy. (Octavo.)

> Reprinted in Paris in 1572, without *Les Douze Reigles*, edition shared by Galliot du Pré and Vincent Norment. Avec Privilege du Roy.
> Reprinted in Paris in 1579, edition shared by Jean Borel and Gabriel Buon.
> Reprinted in Lyon: Barthélemy Vincent, 1596, 1605, 1618.

———*Arrestum sive placitum Parlamenti Tholosani, Continens Historiam (in casu matrimoniali) admodum memorabilem adeoque prodigiosam: unà cum centum elegantissimis atque doctissimis Annotationibus Clariss. I. C. Dn. Ioan. Corasii ... Doctiss. Viro Hugone Suraeo Gallo interprete.* Frankfurt: Andreas Wechel, 1576.

Reprinted in Frankfurt: Heirs Wechel, Claude Marnius and Jean Aubry, 1588.

Guillaume Le Sueur, *Admiranda historia de Pseudo Martino Tholosae Damnato Idib. Septemb. Anno Domini MDLX Ad Michaelum Fabrum ampliss. in supremo Tholosae Senatu Praesidem.* Lyon: Jean de Tournes, 1561. "A Gulielmo Sudario Boloniensi Latinitate donatum" (p. 2); "colligeb. G. le Sueur Bolon" (p. 22). Bibliothèque Nationale, F13876.

————*Histoire Admirable d'un Faux et Supposé Mary, advenue en Languedoc, l'an mil cinq cens soixante.* Paris: Vincent Sertenas, 1561. Avec privilege du Roy.

Two printings of this pamphlet came out the same year, one with the title spelled as above (Bibliothèque Mazarine, 47214), the other with *Histoire* misspelled *Histoite* (Bibliothèque Nationale, Rés. Ln^{27} 9277 bis). The reprinting of this work by Edouard Fournier in his *Variétés historiques et littéraires* (Paris, 1867, vol. 8, pp. 99–118) is misdated, full of errors and editorial additions, and omits four pages of the text.

————*Histoire admirable d'Arnaud Tilye, lequel emprunta faussement le nom de Martin Guerre, afin de jouir de sa femme.* Lyon: Benoît Rigaud, 1580.

————*Histoire admirable du faux et supposé mary, arrivée à une femme notable au pays de Languedoc en ces derniers troubles.* Paris: Jean Mestais, no date [ca. 1615].

Jean Papon, *Recueil d'Arrests Notables des Courts Souveraines de France ... Nouvellement reveuz et augmentez outre les precedents impressions, de plusieurs arrests.* Paris: Nicolas Chesneau, 1565, ff. 452^v–456^v.

Henri Estienne, *Herodoti Halicarnassei historiae lib. ix ... . Henr. Stephani pro Herodotu.* Geneva: Henri Estienne for Ulrich Fugger, 1566, f. **** ii^r.

————*L'Introduction au traité de la conformité des merveilles anciennes avec les modernes. Ou traité prepartatif à L'Apologie pour Herodote.* Geneva: Henri Estienne, 1566. Au lecteur.

Gilbert Cousin, *Narrationum sylva qua Magna Rerum, partim à casu fortunaque, partim à divina humanaque mente evenientium . . . Lib VIII.* Basel: Henricpetrina, 1567. Pp. 610-611: "Impostura Arnauldi Tillii."

François de Belleforest, *Histoires prodigieuses, extraictes de plusieurs fameux Autheurs, Grecs et Latins, sacrez et Prophanes, divisees en deux Tomes. Le premier mis en lumiere par P. Boaistuau . . . Le second par Claude de Tesserant, et augmenté de dix histoires par François de Belle-Forest Comingeois.* Paris: Jean de Bordeaux, 1571. Vol. 2, f. 282^{r-v}: "Faux Martin à Thoulouze."

> Subsequent editions include Paris, 1574, Antwerp, 1594, and Paris, 1598.

Antoine Du Verdier, *Les Diverses lecons d'Antoine Du Verdier . . . Contenans plusieurs histoires, discours, et faicts memorables.* Lyon: Barthélemy Honorat, 1577. Book 4, ch. 26.

Pierre Grégoire, *Syntagma Iuris Universi . . . Authore Petro Gregorio Tholosano I. V. Doctore et professore publico in Academia Tholosana.* Lyon: Antoine Gryphius, 1582. Part III, book 36, ch. 6, "On the crime of adultery," p. 669.

Michel de Montaigne, *Essais,* Paris, 1588. Book 3, ch. 11, "Des boyteux."

——*The Essayes or Morall, Politike and Millitarie Discourses of Lord Michael de Montaigne . . . done into English by . . . John Florio.* London, 1610. Book 3, ch. 11, "Of the Lame or Cripple."

Auger Gaillard, *Les Amours prodigieuses d'Augier Gaillard, rodier de Rabastens en Albigeois, mises en vers françois et en langue albigeoise . . . Imprimé nouvellement.* [Béarn], 1592.

> Modern edition by Ernest Nègre in the *Oeuvres complètes.* Paris, 1970. Pp. 514, 525-526.

Géraud de Maynard, *Notables et singulieres Questions du Droict Escrit: Decidees et Iugees par Arrests Memorables de la Cour souveraine du Parlement de Tholose.* Paris, 1628, pp. 500-507. This work first appeared in 1603.

Jacques-Auguste de Thou, *Historiarum sui temporis ab anno Domini 1543 usque ad annum 1607 Libri CXXXVIII.* Orléans [Geneva]: Pierre de la Roviere, 1620. Vol. 1, p. 788.

> The story of Martin Guerre did not appear in the first edition (1604) of this famous history by the Parlementaire of Paris, de Thou. After the 1609 edition, he wrote out an addition on

the case (bound in to vol. 4 of the 1609 edition in the Réserve at the Bibliothèque Nationale, between pp. 288 and 289); and it was finally printed in 1620 after his death as part of book 26.

————*Histoire de Monsieur de Thou, Des choses arrivées de son temps. Mise en François par P. du Ryer.* Paris, 1659. Vol. 2, pp. 177-178.

Estienne Pasquier, *Les Recherches de la France.* Paris: L. Sonnius, 1621. Book 6, ch. 35.

Jacob Cats, *S'weerelts Begin, Midden, Eynde, Besloten in den Trou-ringh Met den Proef-steen van den Selven door I. Cats . . . Trou-geval sonder exempel, Geschiet, in Vranckryck, In het Iaer MDLIX,* in *Alle de Wercken, Amsterdam,* 1658.

The prolific Dutch moralist tells the story of Martin Guerre in rhymed couplets.

Jean Baptiste de Rocoles, *Les imposteurs insignes ou Histoires de plusieurs hommes de néant, de toutes Nations, qui ont usurpé la qualité d'Empereurs, Roys et Princes . . . Par Jean Baptiste de Rocoles, Historiographe de France et de Brandebourg.* Amsterdam: Abraham Wolfgang, 1683. Chapter 18: "L'Imposteur Mary, Arnaud du Thil, Archi-fourbe."

Rocoles explains that, though in principle his book is confined to impostors who tried to steal scepters and crowns, he is making an exception for this case because it is so "memorable and prodigious." He is following Coras's account, he says, making changes only where "the rudeness of the language" would no longer be permitted by "the politeness of the day" (p. 287).

————German translation, *Geschichte merkwürdiger Betrüger,* Halle, 1761. Vol. 1, pp. 419-445.

Germaine Lafaille, *Annales de la ville de Toulouse.* Toulouse, 1687–1701. Pt. 2, pp. 198-199.

F. Gayot de Pitaval, *Causes célèbres et intéressantes.* Paris, 1734. Vol. 1, ch. 1.

New edition, revised by M. Richer, Amsterdam, 1772.

One of the most interesting retellings of the case of Martin Guerre, and the only one to speculate freely on the possibility that Bertrande was the accomplice of Arnaud du Tilh: "Many people will believe that Bertrande de Rols helped deceive herself because the error pleased her." The impostor could never have shown all the tiny gestures special to the original.

English translation without commentary by the novelist Charlotte Turner Smith as one of fifteen cases taken from Gayot de Pitival and Richer in *The Romance of Real Life*. London: T. Cadell, 1787. Vol. 2, ch. 4: "The pretended Martin Guerre." First American edition, Philadelphia: J. Carey, 1799. Pp. 202-221.

Charles Hubert, *Le Faux Martinguerre, ou La Famille d'Artigues, Mélodrame en Trois Actes, À Grand Spectacle, Tiré des Causes Célèbres ... Représenté pour la première fois à Paris, sur la théâtre de la Gaieté, le 23 août 1808*. Paris: Barba, 1808.

Reprinted, Paris, 1824.

So romanticized as to be unrecognizable: "Martinguerre" is a count who has been away in the Indies; Arnaud du Tilh is unmasked by his own father, etc.

Pierre Larousse, *Grand dictionnaire universel*. Paris, 1865 1890. Vol. 8, p. 1603: "Guerre, Martin, gentilhomme gascon."

Celebrated Claimants Ancient and Modern. London: Chatto and Windus, 1873. Pp. 84-90.

L'Abbé P. Haristoy, *Galerie Basque de Personnages de Renom* in *Recherches historiques sur le pays Basque*. Bayonne, 1884. Vol. 2, ch. 24: "Martin Aguerre de Hendaye."

Armand Praviel, *L'Incroyable Odyssée de Martin Guerre*. Paris: Librairie Gallimard, 1933.

Janet Lewis, *The Wife of Martin Guerre*. San Francisco, 1941. French edition, *La Femme de Martin Guerre*. Paris: Editions R. Laffont, 1947. Lewis based her novel on a nineteenth-century English report of the case. She tells about how her views have changed as a result of reading Coras in *The Triquarterly*, 55 (Fall 1982), 104-110.

Addenda

Jean de Coras, *Processo, et Arresto ò sentenza data dal Parlamento di Tolosa sopra d'un fatto prodiogoso et memorabile, tradotto di lingua francese nella favella toscana, per Mag. Gio. Batt* Forteguerri Dott*re* Pistorese, con cento annotationi ornate et aggiunte da lui*. Dedication of Forteguèrri to Christine de Lorraine, Grand-Duchess of Tuscany, dated Pistoia, April 1591. (Manuscript described by H. P. Kraus, Rare Books and Manuscripts, List 203, no. 132.) Forteguèrri has translated the 1561 edition of the *Arrest Memorable*, occasionally adding his own annotations to those of Coras.

Notes

····►◄◆►◄····

The following abbreviations and short forms are used in the notes. References to the Inventaires-Sommaires of the various departmental archives will be indicated by the letter *I* placed before the abbreviation.

ACArt	Archives communales d'Artigat
ADAr	Archives départementales de l'Ariège
ADGe	Archives départementales du Gers
ADGi	Archives départementales de la Gironde
ADHG	Archives départementales de la Haute-Garonne
ADPC	Archives départmentales du Pas-de-Calais
ADPyA	Archives départementales des Pyrénées-Atlantiques
ADR	Archives départementales du Rhône
AN	Archives Nationales
Coras	Jean de Coras, *Arrest Memorable du Parlement de Tholose. Contenant Une Histoire prodigieuse d'un supposé mary, advenüe de nostre temps: enrichie de cent et onze belles et doctes annotations* (Paris: Galliot du Pré, 1572)
Le Sueur, *Historia*	Guillaume Le Sueur, *Admiranda historia de Pseudo Martino Tholosae Damnato Idib. Septemb. Anno Domini MDLX* (Lyon: Jean de Tournes, 1561)
Le Sueur, *Histoire*	Guillaume Le Sueur, *Histoire Admirable d'un Faux et Supposé Mary, advenue en Languedoc, l'an mil cinq cens soixante* (Paris: Vincent Sertenas, 1561)

⋯•———◆———•⋯

Note regarding dates: Until 1564, the new year in France was dated from Easter Sunday. In the text all dates are given by our reckoning. In the notes, any date before Easter is given in both reckonings, e.g., January 15, 1559/60.

Introduction

1. Jean Gilles de Noyers, *Proverbia Gallicana* (Lyon: Jacques Mareschal, 1519–20), C ii^v; "Ioannis Aegidii Nuceriensis Adagiorum Gallis vulgarium ... traductio," in *Thresor de la langue francoyse* (Paris, 1606), pp. 2, 6, 19; James Howell, "Some Choice Proverbs ... in the French Toung,"in *Lexicon Tetraglotton* (London, 1660), p. 2.

2. Among other studies, see Jean-Louis Flandrin, *Les Amours paysans, XVIe-XIXe siècles* (Paris, 1970), and *Familles. Parenté, maison, sexualité dans l'ancienne société* (Paris, 1976); J. M. Gouesse, "Parenté, famille et mariage en Normandie aux XVIIe et XVIIIe siècles," *Annales: Economies, Sociétés, Civilisations*, 27 (1972), 1139–54; André Burguière, "Le Rituel du mariage en France: Pratiques ecclésiastiques et pratiques populaires (XVIe-XVIIIe siècles)," ibid., 33 (1978), pp. 637–649; Alain Croix, *La Bretagne aux 16e et 17e siècles: La Vie, la mort, la foi* (2 vols., Paris, 1981); Jacques Le Goff and Jean-Claude Schmitt, eds., *Le Charivari: Actes de la table ronde organisée à Paris (25–27 avril 1977) par l'Ecole des Hautes Etudes en Sciences Sociales et le Centre National de la Recherche Scientifique* (Paris, 1981).

3. Thomas Platter, *Autobiographie,* tr. Marie Helmer (Cahier des Annales, 22; Paris, 1964), p. 51.

4. Jacques Peletier, *L'Art poëtique de Jacques Peletier du Mans (1555),* ed. J. Boulanger (Paris, 1930), pp. 186–189; Coras, pp. 146–147. *Les Cent Nouvelles Nouvelles,* ed. Thomas Wright (Paris, 1858), conte 35. Noël du Fail, *Les Propos Rustiques: Texte original de 1547,* ed. Arthur de la Borderie (Paris, 1878; Geneva: Slatkine Reprints, 1970), pp. 43–44.

5. Emmanuel Le Roy Ladurie, *Montaillou, village occitan de 1294 à 1324* (Paris, 1975); English translation, *Montaillou: The Promised Land of Error,* by Barbara Bray (New York, 1978). Carlo Ginzburg,

Il Formaggio e i vermi: Il Cosmo di un mugnaio del '500 (Turin, 1976); English translation, *The Cheese and the Worms: The Cosmos of a Six-teenth-Century Miller,* by John and Anne Tedeschi (Baltimore, 1980). Michael M. Sheehan, "The Formation and Stability of Marriage in Fourteenth-Century England," *Mediaeval Studies,* 32 (1971), 228–263, Jean-Louis Flandrin, *Le Sexe et l'Occident* (Paris, 1981), ch. 4.

6. AN, JJ248, 80^{r-v}. Alfred Soman, "Deviance and Criminal Justice in Western Europe, 1300–1800: An Essay in Structure," *Criminal Justice History: An International Annual,* 1 (1980), 1–28.

7. Coras, pp. 146–147. On the editions of the *Arrest Memorable,* see my bibliography.

8. According to Le Sueur, the Guerres established a tileworks at Artigat (*Historia,* p. 3); this tileworks is found in 1594 among the family properties (ADHG, B, Insinuations, vol. 6, 96^{v}). Le Sueur stated that Bertrande de Rols and Pierre Guerre had been put in prison (p. 11); this was ordered by the Parlement of Toulouse (ADHG, B, La Tournelle, vol. 74, May 20, 1560; vol. 76, September 12, 1560).

1. From Hendaye to Artigat

1. Pierre de Lancre, *Tableau de l'inconstance des mauvais anges et demons* (Bordeaux, 1612), pp. 32–38, 44–45. ADPyA, 1J160, no. 45, March 9, 1609, for the "S^{r} de la maison" in Hendaye and nearby Ur-rugne. James A. Tuck and Robert Grenier, "A 16th-Century Basque Whaling Station in Labrador," *Scientific American,* 245 (November 1981), 125–136; William A. Douglass and Jon Bilbao, *Amerikanuak: Basques in the New World* (Reno, 1975), pp. 51–59. Jean-Pierre Pous-sou, "Recherches sur l'immigration bayonnaise et basque à Bordeaux au XVIIIe siècle," *De l'Adour au Pays Basque. Actes du XXIe Congrès d'études régionales tenu à Bayonne, les 4 et 5 mai 1968*(Bayonne, 1971), pp. 67–79. Jean-François Soulet, *La Vie quotidienne dans les Pyrénées sous l'Ancien Régime* (Paris, 1974), pp. 220–225. William A. Doug-lass, *Echalar and Murélaga* (London, 1975), ch. 3.

2. Philippe Veyrin, *Les Basques de Labourd, de Soule et de Basse-Na-varre* (Bayonne, 1947), pp. 39ff. L. Dassance, "Propriétés collectives

et biens communaux dans l'ancien pays de Labourd,"*Gure Herria,* 29 (1957), 129-138. Davydd J. Greenwood, *Unrewarding Wealth. The Commercialization and Collapse of Agriculture in a Spanish Basque Town* (Cambridge, Eng.,1976), ch. 1. Paul Courteault, "De Hendaye à Bayonne en 1528," *Gure Herria,* 3 (1923), 273-277. On the increased population of Hendaye by 1598, see ADPyA, 1J160, no. 46, April 3, 1598. De Lancre, pp. 45-46.

3. E. Dravasa, "Les privilèges des Basques du Labourd sous l'Ancien Régime" (thesis for the doctorate, University of Bordeaux, Faculty of Law, 1950), pp. 28-29. ADGi, 1B10, 21^v-22^r. ADPyA, 1J160, no. 45, May 19, 1552. De Lancre, pp. 33-34, 42.

4. "Coutumes générales gardées et observées au Pays de Labourd," in P. Haristoy, *Recherches historiques sur le Pays Basque* (Bayonne and Paris, 1884), vol. 2, pp. 458-461; the Fors of Labourd were written down in 1513. Jacques Poumarède, *Recherches sur les successions dans le sud-ouest de la France au Moyen Age* (thesis for the doctorate, University of Toulouse, 1968), pp. 315-320.

5. On this whole region, see Léon Dutil, *L'Etat économique du Languedoc à la fin de l'Ancien Régime* (Paris, 1911); Philippe Wolff, *Commerces et marchands de Toulouse, vers 1350-vers 1450* (Paris, 1954); Michel Chevalier, *La Vie humaine dans les Pyrénées ariégeoises* (Paris, 1956); Gilles Caster, *Le Commerce du pastel et de l'épicerie à Toulouse, 1450-1561* (Toulouse, 1962); E. Le Roy Ladurie, *Les Paysans de Languedoc* (Paris, 1966); Soulet, *Vie quotidienne;* and John Mundy, "Village, Town and City in the Region of Toulouse," in J. A. Raftis, ed., *Pathways to Medieval Peasants* (Papers in Mediaeval Studies, 2; Toronto: Pontifical Institute of Mediaeval Studies, 1981), pp. 141-190.

6. Jean Froissart, *Chroniques,* ed. Léon Mirot (Paris, 1931), vol. 12, pp. 21-24, book 3, par., 6. ADHG, C1925; 3E15289, 328^r. ADAr, G271; 30J^2, Reconnaissance of 1679; 5E6653, 188^r-189^r, 200$^{r\text{-}v}$; 5E6655, 14^r-16^r.

7. ADAr, 5E6653, 9^v, 96^r-97^r, 101^v-102^v, 142$^{r\text{-}v}$, 200$^{r\text{-}v}$; 5E6655, 1^v-2^v, 8$^{r\text{-}v}$, 32$^{r\text{-}v}$, 98^r; 5E6656, 12^r; 5E6847, December 17, 1562. For the contract of "gasailhe" and all other customs in this region, see Paul Cayla, *Dictionnaire des institutions, des coutumes, et de la langue en usage dans quelques pays de Languedoc de 1535 à 1648* (Montpellier,

1964). On Le Carla and nearby, see Elisabeth Labrousse, *Pierre Bayle* (The Hague, 1963), ch. 1.

8. Nineteen testaments drawn from ADAr, 5E5335, 6219, 6220, 6221, 6223, 6224, 6653, 6655, 6859, 6860; ADHG, 3E15280, 15983. ADAr, 5E6860, 110^v–111^v; ACArt, Terrier of 1651. ADAr, 5E6220, October 8, 1542; 5E8169, March 12, 1541/42.

9. ADAr, 5E6223, December 10, 1528; 5E6653, 95^v–96^r; 5E6860, 12^r–13^v, 74^r–76^r.

10. ADAr, 5E6653, 95^v–97^r, 201^v–202^r; 5E6846, 34^v–36^v; 30J^2, reconnaissance of 1679; ADHG, B50 (arrêts civils), 678^v–679^v; B, Insinuations, vol. 6, 96^v.

11. ADAr, 5E6653, 1^{r-v}, 96^v–97^r; 5E6655, 29^r, 35^r, 158^v; 5E6656, 12^r, 26^v; 5E6837, 126^r–127^v; 5E6846, 34^v–36^v; ADHG, 2G134, 2G143; 2G108, p. 263.

12. ADAr, 30J^2, Inventaire pour les consuls . . . d'Artigat, 1639; Reconnaissance of 1679; ADHG, 2G203, no. 1; C1925. ADAr, 5E6860, 12^r–13^v. ADHG, 2G108, 127^r, 151^r–152^r. F. Pasquier, "Coutumes du Fossat dans le Comté de Foix d'après une charte de 1274," *Annales du Midi,* 9 (1897), 257–322; ADAr, 5E6654.

13. "Coutumes . . . observées au Pays de Labourd," p. 482. ADPyA, 1J160, no. 4, January 14, 1550/51, no. 3, June 12, 1559. F. Pasquier, *Donation du fief de Pailhès en 1258 et documents concernant les seigneurs de cette baronnie au XVIe siècle* (Foix, 1980). ADAr, 2G203, no. 8.

14. Pierre Bec, *Les Interférences linguistiques entre Gascon et Languedocien dans les parlers du Comminges et du Couserans* (Paris, 1968), pp. 74–75. Pasquier, *Pailhès,* p. 3. Léon Dutil, *La Haute-Garonne et sa région* (Toulouse, 1928), ch. 14. ADHG, 2G108, pp. 261ff. J. Decap, *Le Diocèse de Rieux avant la Révolution* (Foix, 1898). The diocese of Rieux was established in 1318 and ended with the Revolution.

15. Le Sueur, *Historia,* p. 3; *Histoire,* A ii^r. Coras, p. 150. ADHG, B, Insinuations, vol. 6, 95^v–97^v. ACArt, Terrier of 1651, 34^r–41^r, 209^r, 290^r, 310^r.

16. Veyrin, pp. 43, 263. De Lancre, pp. 42–44. ADPyA, 1J160, no. 45, August 18, 1598; no. 46, January 14, 1620.

17. Coras, pp. 55–56. G. Brunet, *Poésies basques de Bernard Dechepare . . . d'après l'édition de Bordeaux, 1545* (Bordeaux, 1847). ADGi, 1B10, 21^v–22^r, royal letters in French for the parishes of Urrugne and

Hendaye; Dravasa, p. 125; ADPyA, 1J160, no. 3, testaments of the seigniorial house of Urtubie in Gascon (1493) and in French (1559); no other families from Hendaye or Urrugne left written wills. ADAr, 5E6223 (contracts in French in 1528); 5E8169 (marriage contract in Occitan, March 12, 1541). ADAr, 5E6653, 96^r–102^v. ADHG, 2G207 (the first schoolmaster sent to Artigat, July 2, 1687).

18. ADAr, 5E6223, December 10, 1528; 5E6653, 95^v; 5E6654, 24$^{r\text{-}v}$; 5E6655, 29^r; 5E8169, March 12, 1541/42. ACArt, Registre des Mariages de la Paroisse d'Artigat, 1632–1649. ADHG, 3E15983, 126^r–127^r. One can even find a Pierre de Guerre alias Le Basque serving as a domestic to the seignior of Vaudreuille, many miles northeast of the diocese of Rieux (AN, JJ262, 245^v–247^v).

19. Le Sueur, *Historia,* p. 3; *Histoire,* A ii^v.

20. Seventeen contracts of marriage and two bequests for dowries drawn from ADAr, 5E5335, 6220, 6653, 6656, 6837, 6838, 8169; ADHG, 3E15280, 15983. The highest dowry given here is 50 écus (about 150 livres), given in 1542 to a shoemaker of Le Mas-d'Azil. For a contrast with passing of lands to sons later in the century, compare the donation of the rural merchant Jean Cazalz of Le Fossat to his son in 1585: two properties and a promise of 2000 écus in cash, a house, and furniture on the day of his marriage (ADHG, B, Insinuations, vol. 1, 563^v–565^r). Cayla, pp. 236–237. ADHG, B, Insinuations, vol. 6, 95^v–97^v.

21. ADHG, 2G108, p. 263. Coras, p. 61. A. Moulis, "Les Fiançailles et le mariage dans les Pyrénées centrales et spécialement dans l'Ariège," *Bulletin annuel de la société ariégoise des sciences, lettres et arts,* 22 (1966), 74–80.

2. The Discontented Peasant

1. Coras, p. 40.

2. ADAr, 5E6654, 37^r. In the many contracts I have examined from Le Mas-d'Azil through the Lèze valley, I have found only one Martin before 1561, a former tenant of the seignior of Saint-Martin-d'Oydes (ADAr, E182, Reconnaissance of 1549, 50^r). Compare the many men named Martin, Martissantz, and Marticot in the area of

Hendaye, ADPyA, 1J160, no. 4, January 14, 1550/51, March 5, 1554/55; no. 45, August 18, 1598. "Proverbes françoys," in *Thresor de la langue francoyse*, p. 23; "L'Ours 'Martin' d'Ariège," *Bulletin annuel de la société ariégoise des sciences, lettres et arts*, 2 (1966), 137–139, 170–172.

3. Coras, pp. 2–4, 40–43, 53, 76. ADHG, B, La Tournelle, vol. 74, May 20, 1560. Hierosme de Monteux, *Commentaire de la conservation de la santé* (Lyon, 1559), pp. 202–203. De Lancre, *Tableau de l'inconstance*, pp. 38, 41, 47; Soulet, *Vie quotidienne*, pp. 228–232, 279. A. Esmein, *Le Mariage en droit canonique* (Paris, 1891), pp. 239–247.

4. G. Doublet, "Un Diocèse pyrénéen sous Louis XIV: La Vie populaire dans la vallée de l'Ariège sous l'épiscopat de F.-E. de Caulet (1645–1680)," *Revue des Pyrénées*, 7 (1895), 379–380; Xavier Ravier, "Le Charivari en Languedoc occidental," in Le Goff and Schmitt, eds., *Le Charivari*, pp. 411–428.

5. Le Sueur, *Historia*, p. 12. Coras, pp. 40, 44.

6. Le Sueur, *Historia*, p. 17. Coras, pp. 145–146.

7. Le Roy Ladurie, *Montaillou*, ch. 7.

8. ADAr, 5E6220, front cover, with whimsical pictures of soldiers; 5E6653, 1^v, 95^v–96^r; 5E6656, 11^r, 50^r; 5E6847, December 12, 1562; 5E6860, 110^v–111^v. Roger Doucet, *Les Institutions de la France au XVIe siècle* (Paris, 1948), pp. 632–641. Veyrin, *Les Basques*, p. 138. J. Nadal and E. Giralt, *La Population catalane de 1553 à 1717: L'Immigration française* (Paris, 1960), pp. 67–74, 315.

9. Coras, p. 5. Le Sueur, *Historia*, p. 4. De Lancre, p. 41.

10. ADPyA, 1J160, no. 4, March 5, 1554/55. April 1, 1555. Coras, p. 137.

11. Paul Jacob Hiltpold, "Burgos in the Reign of Philip II: The Ayuntamiento, Economic Crisis and Social Control, 1550–1660" (Ph.D. thesis, University of Texas at Austin, 1981), ch. 2. Henrique Florez, *España Sagrada* (Madrid, 1771), vol. 26, pp. 427–432. Nicolás López Martínez, "El Cardenal Mendoza y la Reforma Tridentina en Burgos," *Hispania Sacra*, 16 (1963), 61–121.

12. Le Sueur, *Historia*, p. 4. Coras, p. 137. E. Lemaire, Henri Courteault et al., *La Guerre de 1557 en Picardie* (Saint-Quentin, 1896), vol. 1, pp. ccxxi–ccxv, vol. 2, pp. 48, 295.

3. The Honor of Bertrande de Rols

1. ADAr, 5E6653, 95^v–98^r; 5E6655, 110^v–111^v.
2. ADHG, 2G108, 127^r. Doublet, "Un Diocèse pyrénéen," pp. 369–371. Coras, p. 44. Henry Institoris and Jacques Sprenger, *Malleus maleficarum,* tr. Montague Summers (London, 1948), p. 55, part I, question 8.
3. Coras, pp. 40–41.
4. ADAr, 5E6654, 29^r; 5E6655, 79^r; 5E6838, 104^v.
5. ADAr, 5E5335, 92^{r-v}, 135^r, 282^v–283^r; 5E6653, 6^r; 5E6654, 29^r; 5E6655, 6^{r-v}, 106^v–107^r, 137^v–138^r; 5E6656, 58^r; E182, 26^r. ADHG, 3E15280, January 14, 1547/48. Jacques Beauroy, *Vin et société à Bergerac du Moyen Age aux temps modernes* (Stanford French and Italian Studies, 4, Saratoga, Calif., 1976), p. 125.
6. Cayla, *Dictionnaire,* pp. 54 58, 236. ADAr, 5E6219, July 31, 1540; 5E6653, 3^{r-v}, 54^v, 5E6655, 117^v. ADHG, 3E15280, January 31, 1547/48; 3E15983, 126^r–127^r, 322^r–334^v.
7. ADAr, 5E6846, 34^v–36^v; ADHG, B50 (arrêts civils), 678^v–679^v. Le Roy Ladurie, *Montaillou, village occitan,* pp. 286–287. ADAr, 5E6837, 236^r–237^r; 5E6655, 110^v–111^v; 5E6847, September 23, 1562. Pasquier, "Coutumes du Fossat," pp. 298–299; Cayla, p. 63.
8. De Lancre, *Tableau de l'inconstance,* pp. 42–44. For a later portrait of the Labourd women, see G. Olphe-Galliard, *Un Nouveau type particulariste ébauché. Le Paysan basque de Labourd à travers les âges* (La Science Sociale suivant la méthode d'observation, 20; Paris, 1905), pp. 437–441.
9. Le Sueur, *Historia,* p. 9. ADAr, 5E6223, July 5, 1542; 5E6224, January 6, 1547/48. By the late 1550s Martin Guerre's inheritance and all the revenues from it for eight years were estimated at 7000–8000 livres (Coras, p. 29).
10. Coras, pp. 5–7, 25; Jean de Coras, *Opera omnia* (Wittenberg, 1603), vol. 1, pp. 730–731. Jean Dauvillier, *Le Mariage dans le droit classique de l'Eglise* (Paris, 1933), pp. 304–307. Bernard de La Roche-Flavin, *Arrests Notables du Parlement de Tolose* (Lyon, 1619), pp. 601–602.
11. Coras, p. 46.

12. ADHG, B38 (arrêts civils), 60^v–61^r; B47 (arrêts civils), 487^r; 2G241.

13. Coras, pp. 1, 5, 7.

4. The Masks of Arnaud du Tilh

1. Coras, pp. 8, 151. François de Belleforest, *La Cosmographie uni-verselle de tout le monde . . . Auteur en partie Munster . . augmentée . . . par François de Belle-forest Comingeois* (Paris: Michel Sonnius, 1575), pp. 368–372.

2. ADHG, B78 (arrêts civils), 3^r–4^r; IADHG, BB58, ff. 220, 214. Charles Higounet, *Le Comté de Comminges de ses origines à son annexion à la couronne* (Toulouse, 1949), vol. 1, pp. 277, 292. ADGe, 3E1570, July 10, 1557; 3E1569, July 27, 1552.

3. Higounet, pp. 512ff.; Wolff, *Commerces et marchands de Toulouse,* carte 12. ADGe, 3E1569, December 19, 1551; 3E1570, April 7 and July 4, 1557. ADHG, 4E2016, 4E1568, 2E2403. Georges Couarraze, *Au pays du Savès: Lombez évêché rural, 1317–1801* (Lombez, 1973).

4. ADGe, G332, 47^r–48^r; 3E1570, April 21, 1557. Coras, pp. 97, 151.

5. Coras, pp. 52, 54. ADGe, G332, 47bis^{r-v}.

6. Coras, pp. 56–57, 77, 97. Leah Otis, "Une Contribution à l'étude du blasphème au bas Moyen Age," in *Diritto comune e diritti locali nella storia dell' Europa. Atti del Convegno di Varenna, 12–15 giugno 1979* (Milan, 1980), pp. 213–223. IADHG, B1900, f. 118, B1901, f. 143 (royal ordinances on blasphemy of 1493, 1523).

7. Raymond de Beccarie de Pavie, Sieur de Fourquevaux, *The In-structions sur le Faict de la Guerre,* ed. G. Dickinson (London, 1954), pp. xxix–xxxii. ADGe, 3E1571, April 16, 1558, and passim. Coras, pp. 53, 57, 144. Yves-Marie Bercé, "Les Gascons à Paris aux XVIe et XVIIe siècles," *Bulletin de la société de l'histoire de Paris et de l'Ile-de-France,* 106 (1979), 23–29.

8. Coras, pp. 8–11, 38–39, 144.

9. *Le Grand Calendrier et compost des Bergers avec leur astrologie* (Troyes: Jean Lecoq, 154[1]), M i^r–M iii^r.

10. Coras, p. 53.

11. Le Sueur, *Historia,* p. 13; *Histoire,* C iv^v. Coras, pp. 144–146. François de Rabutin, *Commentaires des dernieres guerres en la Gaule Belgique, entre Henry second du nom, très-chrestien Roy de France et Charles Cinquiesme, Empereur, et Philippe son fils, Roy d'Espaigne* (1574), books 4–5 in *Nouvelle Collection des Mémoires pour servir à l'histoire de France,* ed. Michaud and Poujoulat (Paris, 1838), vol. 7.

12. Coras, pp. 145–147; Le Sueur, *Historia,* p. 22.

13. ADGe, 3E1569, December 19, 1551.

14. Bibliothèque Nationale, Département des Estampes, *Inventaire du fonds français. Graveurs du seizième siècle,* vol. 2, L-W by Jean Adhémar, p. 273: "L'Histoire des Trois Frères." ADR, BP443, 37^r–39^v, 294^v–296^r.

5. The Invented Marriage

1. Le Sueur, *Historia,* pp. 5–7; *Histoire,* B i^v–B ii^v. Coras, p. 63.

2. Mark Snyder and Seymour Uranowitz, "Reconstructing the Past: Some Cognitive Consequences of Person Perception," *Journal of Personality and Social Psychology,* 36 (1978), 941–950. Mark Snyder and Nancy Cantor, "Testing Hypotheses about Other People: The Use of Historical Knowledge," *Journal of Experimental Psychology,* 15 (1979), 330–342.

3. Etienne Pasquier, *Les Recherches de la France* (Paris: L. Sonnius, 1621), pp. 571–572.

4. Coras, p. 25; Le Sueur, *Historia,* p. 7.

5. Coras, pp. 68, 34, 65–66. Le Sueur, *Histoire,* C i^v, C iii^r.

6. Coras, p. 149. Le Roy Ladurie, *Montaillou, village occitan,* p. 275, n. 1.

7. Sheehan, "The Formation and Stability of Marriage," pp. 228–263. J. M. Turlan, "Recherches sur le mariage dans la pratique coutumière (XIIe–XVIe s.)," *Revue historique de droit français et étranger,* 35 (1957), 503–516. Beatrice Gottlieb, "The Meaning of Clandestine Marriage," in Robert Wheaton and Tamara K. Hareven, eds., *Family and Sexuality in French History* (Philadelphia, 1980), pp. 49–83.

8. Jean-Jacques de Lescazes, *Le Memorial historique, contenant la narration des troubles et ce qui est arrivé diversement de plus remarquable*

dans le Païs de Foix et Diocese de Pamies (Toulouse, 1644), chs. 12–16. Jean Crespin, *Histoire des Martyrs persecutez et mis à mort pour la Verité de l'Evangile* (Toulouse, 1885–1889), vol. 1, p. 457, vol. 3, pp. 646–649. J. Lestrade, *Les Huguenots dans le diocèse de Rieux* (Paris, 1904), pp. 4, 10, 29–30. J. M. Vidal, *Schisme et hérésie au diocèse de Pamiers, 1467–1626* (Paris, 1931), pp. 147–169. Raymond Mentzer, "Heresy Proceedings in Languedoc, 1500–1560" (Ph.D. thesis, University of Wisconsin, 1973), ch. 12. Labrousse, *Pierre Bayle,* pp. 6–8. Alice Wemyss, *Les Protestants du Mas-d'Azil* (Toulouse, 1961), pp. 17–25. Paul-F. Geisendorf, *Livres des habitants de Genève, 1549–1560* (Geneva, 1957–1963), vol. 1, pp. 9, 13. ADAr, 5E6654, 5^r, 16^v, 29^r. ADHG, 2G108, 127^r–130^v; B422 (arrêts civils), October 22, 1620.

9. ADHG, B33 (arrêts civils), 156^v–157^r; B38 (arrêts civils), 60^r–61^r; B47 (arrêts civils), 487^r; ADAr, 5E6655, 14^r–16^r.

10. ACArt, Terrier of 1651, 137^r–139^v. "Memoire des personnes decedees en la ville du Carla en Foix ou en sa Jurisdiction commance le vingt et deusiesme octobre 1642," 10^r, 12^v, 13^r, 13^v (records kept by Jean Bayle, pastor of the Reformed Church of Le Carla from 1637 to 1685; photocopy in the possession of Elisabeth Labrousse).

11. Couarraze, *Lombez,* p. 122. ADHG, B, La Tournelle, vol. 74, May 20, 1560.

12. Le Sueur, *Historia,* pp. 16, 21–22. Coras, p. 160.

13. "Projet d'ordonnance sur les mariages, 10 novembre 1545," in Jean Calvin, *Opera quae supersunt omnia,* ed. G. Baum, E. Cunitz, and E. Reuss (Brunswick, 1863–1880), vol. 38, pp. 41–44.

6. Quarrels

1. Coras, p. 61. ADHG, B, La Tournelle, vol. 74, May 20, 1560.

2. Le Roy Ladurie, *Les Paysans de Languedoc,* vol. 1, pp. 302–309. ADAr, 5E6655, 8^{r-v}, 98^r; 5E6656, 12^r, 26^v, 29^r, 58^r; 5E6653, 79^v, 200^{r-v}. ADHG, 2G143, 2G134, Arrentements des benefices du diocèse de Rieux. Coras, pp. 150–152.

3. Le Sueur, *Historia,* p. 7; *Histoire,* B iii^r. Coras, pp. 22–23.

4. Coras, pp. 33–34. "Coutumes . . . observées au Pays de Labourd," pp. 467–468. ADAr, 5E6653, 3^{r-v}, 112^{r-v}; 5E6656, 11^r.

5. Coras, pp. 12, 47, 53. De Lancre, *Tableau de l'inconstance,* p. 41.

6. Coras, pp. 53, 62, 66–67. Regarding Bertrande's brother, documents from Artigat not long after the trial mention Pey Rols alias Colombet, heir of the late father and son Andreu and Barthélemy Rols, and another Rols, his name beginning with an A (the page is torn for the rest) in the entourage of Pierre Guerre (ADAr, 5E6653, 95^v–98^r). It is conceivable that one of the "sons-in-law" of Pierre Guerre was a stepson in our contemporary sense (the terms *gendre* and *beau-fils* are used interchangeably in Coras' text). In this case, Bertrande's brother would have been in agreement with her mother and stepfather against her and the new Martin. On the other hand, Bertrande's brother may simply have been elsewhere during 1559–60.

7. Le Sueur, *Historia,* p. 7. Coras, pp. 46, 53, 61–62. Le Roy Ladurie, *Montaillou, village occitan,* ch. 3. Various acts show the Banquels and the Boëris in connection with each other (ADAr, 5E6653, 95^v–96^r, 186^{r-v}). The Lozes are not so often found in connection with the Banquels, but James Delhure, partner of James Loze, is found witnessing a horse rental by Jean Banquels (ADAr, 5E6653, 200^{r-v}).

8. Coras, p. 54. Le Sueur, *Historia,* p. 8.

9. Coras, p. 21.

10. Le Sueur, *Historia,* p. 8; Coras, p. 68. ADAr, 5E6860, 12^r–13^v; 5E6837, 188^v–189^v. ADHG, 2G143, 1550; B37 (arrêts civils), 68^r. The *lieutenant-criminel* in the Sénéchaussée of Toulouse for the arson case was Jean Rochon, former judge and officer of the Mint in Paris, a man not likely to be overwhelmed by a petty noble from the Lèze valley (IADHG, B1905, f. 125).

11. Or so I interpret the new Martin's claim in January 1559/60 that Bertrande was "in the power of the said Pierre Guerre, living in his house" (Coras, pp. 37, 45, 67). Two houses are mentioned as belonging to the Guerre family: "the house of Martin Guerre" (ADHG, B76, La Tournelle, September 12, 1560; Coras, p. 129; Le Sueur, *Historia,* p. 19) and "the house of Pierre Guerre" (ADAr, 5E6653, 96^r–98^r). I have assumed that these were separate though nearby dwellings (see the disposition of Guerre lands in 1594 [ADHG, Insinuations, vol. 6, 95^v–97^v] and in 1651 [ACArt, *terrier*]), and that following the deeply rooted Basque custom, married couples lived together in the same house only when each contained an heir to the property. Thus Martin Guerre and Bertrande had lived

with the elder Sanxi Guerre; and Pierre Guerre would live with his chosen heiress and her husband and any unmarried daughters he still had. The new Martin would take up residence separately in the old Sanxi's former house, now passed on to the heir. Of course, it is always possible that these customs were ignored and that the new Martin and Pierre Guerre were living in the same house from 1556 through 1559. One can imagine what the atmosphere was like during these quarrels.

12. Le Sueur, *Historia,* p. 8; *Histoire,* B iii^{r-v}. Coras, pp. 68, 86.

13. Coras, pp. 53–54.

14. Coras, pp. 69–70. ADAr, 5E6653, ff. 96^r–97^r. Jean Imbert, *Institutions Forenses, ou practique iudiciaire . . . par M. Ian Imbert Lieutenant criminel du siege royal de Fontenai Lecomte* (Poitiers: Enguilbert de Marnef, 1563), p. 439.

15. Coras, pp. 68–69.

16. On lying, see the special issue of *Daedalus* entitled "Hypocrisy, Illusion and Evasion" (Summer 1979) and "Special Issue on Lying and Deception," *Berkshire Review,* 15 (1980).

17. Coras, p. 19; Jean Benedicti, *La Somme des Pechez* (Paris, 1595), pp. 151–152.

18. Coras, pp. 69–70, 1, 28.

7. The Trial at Rieux

1. ADHG, 3E15289, 46^r–47^r. ADAr 5E6653, 96^r–98^r; 5E6655, 29^r, 79^r.

2. André Viala, *Le Parlement de Toulouse et l'administration royale laïque, 1420–1525 environ* (Albi, 1953), vol. 1, p. 143. IADHG, B1, f. 37; B. 47, f. 805; B58, f. 638; B66, ff. 290, 294; Lastrade, *Les Huguenots,* p. 1.

3. Coras, pp. 28–29, 85; Imbert, *Practique iudiciaire,* pp. 420–421.

4. On criminal justice in France in the sixteenth century, see Imbert, *Practique iudiciaire,* based on the experience of a *lieutenant-criminel;* Pierre Lizet, *Brieve et succincte maniere de proceder tant à l'institution et decision des causes criminelles que civiles et forme d'informer en icelles* (Paris: Vincent Sertenas, 1555), written by a member of the Parlement of Paris; A. Esmein, *Histoire de la procédure criminelle en*

France (Paris, 1882); Bernard Schnapper, "La Justice criminelle rendue par le Parlement de Paris sous le règne de François Ier," *Revue historique du droit français et étranger*, 152 (1974), 252–284; John H. Langbein, *Prosecuting Crime in the Renaissance* (Cambridge, Mass., 1974); Soman, "Criminal Jurisprudence in Ancien-Régime France: The Parlement of Paris in the Sixteenth and Seventeenth Centuries," in *Crime and Criminal Justice in Europe and Canada,* ed. Louis A. Knafla (Waterloo, Ontario, 1981), pp. 43–74. Alfred Soman's essay is appearing, revised and much expanded, as "La Justice criminelle au XVIe-XVIIe siècles: Le Parlement de Paris et les sièges subalternes," in *Actes du 107e Congrès national des Sociétés Savantes (Brest, 1982). Section de Philologie et d'Histoire jusqu'à 1610.*

5. Coras, pp. 38–46. Imbert, pp. 439–474; Lizet, 2^v–26^v. Yves Castan, *Honnêteté et relations sociales en Languedoc, 1715–1780* (Paris, 1974), pp. 94–96.

6. Coras, pp. 46–47, 50–53, 58–61, 63.

7 Nicole Castan, "La Criminalité familiale dans le ressort du Parlement de Toulouse, 1690–1730," in A. Abbiateci et al., *Crimes et criminalité en France, XVIIe-XVIIIe siècles* (Cahiers des Annales, 33; Paris, 1971), pp. 91–107.

8. Coras, pp. 21, 40, 44. Le Sueur, *Historia,* pp. 12–13; *Histoire,* C iii^v–C iv^r.

9. Coras, pp. 37, 65–66. Le Sueur, *Historia,* p. 10; *Histoire,* C i^v.

10. Coras, pp. 38–39, 73.

11. *Recueil Général des anciennes lois françaises,* ed. Isambert et al. (Paris, 1822–1833), vol. 12, p. 633: "Ordonnance sur le fait de la justice," August 1539, no. 162. Langbein, p. 236. Soman, "Criminal Jurisprudence," pp. 60–61, and his forthcoming "Justice criminelle."

12. Coras, p. 29.

13. Imbert, p. 478. Coras, p. 54. Jean Imbert and Georges Levasseur, *Le Pouvoir, les juges et les bourreaux* (Paris, 1972), pp. 172–175. Of 1069 cases of heresy that came before the Parlement of Toulouse in 1510–1560, Raymond Mentzer found that torture was ordered for 27 (2–3 percent); Raymond A. Mentzer, Jr., "Calvinist Propaganda and the Parlement of Toulouse," *Archive for Reformation History,* 68 (1977), 280. Basing himself on a two-year period (1535–36 and 1545–46), Schnapper found that 16.8 percent of the criminal cases being judged by the Parlement of Paris involved an order to torture

("La Justice criminelle," table 5, pp. 263–265). On larger samples of all crimes but heresy coming before the Parlement of Paris in 1539–1542 and 1609–1610, Alfred Soman found 20.4 percent of the appellants tortured for a confession in the first period, and 5.2 percent in the second. For cases of fraud, perjury, and counterfeiting, the percentages were higher than the average in 1539–1542, and zero in 1609–1610. Of 125 cases of torture in 1539–1542, the results are known in 70 cases: six persons confessed; Soman, "Criminal Jurisprudence," table 6 and p. 54, and his forthcoming "Justice criminelle," table 7. For a general study of torture, see John H. Langbein, *Torture and the Law of Proof: Europe and England in the Ancien Régime* (Chicago, 1977).

14. Coras, pp. 28, 47–48. ADR, BP443, 37^r–39^r.

15. Coras, p. 47. Imbert, *Practique iudiciaire,* pp. 504–506. ADHG, B, La Tournelle, vol. 74, April 30, 1560.

8. The Trial at Toulouse

1. On the Parlement of Toulouse, see Viala, *Parlement de Toulouse;* B. Bennassar and B. Tollon, "Le Parlement" in *Histoire de Toulouse,* ed. Philippe Wolff (Toulouse, 1974), pp. 236–245; and Bernard de La Roche-Flavin (long-time judge in the Parlement of Toulouse), *Treize livres des Parlemens de France* (Geneva, 1621). ADHG, B, La Tournelle, vol. 74, April 27 and May 20, 1560. Jean de Coras, *De acqui. possessione Paraphrasis* (Lyon: Michel Parmentier, 1542), A ii^r; *De Ritu Nuptiarum*, dedication, pp. 205–206, in *De Servitutibus Commentarii* (Lyon: Dominique de Portunariis, 1548); *De verborum obligationibus Scholia* (Lyon: Guillaume Rouillé, 1550), title page.

2. La Roche-Flavin, *Parlemens de France,* pp. 34–35, 54. IADHG, B43, f. 707; B51, f. 2; B32, f. 219; B57, f. 466; B55, f. 415; B57, ff. 70, 73; B56, ff. 556–557, 561; B67, ff. 478–479. Mentzer, "Calvinist Propaganda and the Parlement of Toulouse," pp. 268–283. Joan Davies, "Persecution and Protestantism: Toulouse, 1562–1575," *Historical Journal,* 22 (1979), 49.

3. IADHG, B19, f. 8. Coras, p. 1. Le Sueur, *Historia,* p. 16. La Roche-Flavin, *Parlemens de France,* pp. 753–755. ADHG, B, La Tournelle, vol. 74, April 30, 1560.

4. La Roche-Flavin, *Parlemens de France,* p. 260. Viala, pp. 381–385. ADHG, B, La Tournelle, vol. 72, January 29, 1559/60; vol. 73, March 15, 1559/60; vol. 74, February 1, 1559/60, May 31, August 23, 1560.

5. Le Sueur, *Historia,* pp. 11–12; *Histoire,* C ii^r–C iii^r. Coras, p. 47. IADHG, B1900, f. 256. ADHG, B, La Tournelle, vol. 74, May 20, 1560. La Roche-Flavin, *Parlemens de France,* p. 250.

6. Coras, p. 39.

7. Coras, pp. 48, 51, 73. ADHG, B, La Tournelle, vol. 74, May 20, 1560.

8. For example, Coras was not present for the sentencing of heretics on January 29, 1559/60 (B, La Tournelle, vol. 72), on February 1, 1559/60, or on March 1, 1559/60 (ibid., vol. 73), though he was present for sentences pronounced on days before and after

9. Coras, pp. 48–56, 72–74, 76–77. Imbert and Levasseur, *Le Pouvoir,* pp. 163–169. Soman, "Criminal Jurisprudence," pp. 55–56, and his forthcoming "Justice criminelle."

10. Coras, pp. 34–35, 47, 59, 68–70, 85.

11. Coras, pp. 33–36, 62, 69–70. Le Sueur, *Historia,* p. 14.

12. Coras, pp. 59–60, 71–72, 75–79.

13. Coras, p. 87.

9. The Return of Martin Guerre

1. Le Sueur, *Historia,* p. 4; *Histoire,* A iii^r. On the relative success of the military surgeons associated with the Spanish army in Flanders, see Geoffrey Parker, *The Army of Flanders and the Spanish Road, 1567–1659* (Cambridge, Eng., 1972), p. 168. In the seventeenth century a special house was established in Belgium for soldiers who lost their limbs. L. P. Wright, "The Military Orders in Sixteenth and Seventeenth-Century Spanish Society," *Past and Present,* 43 (May 1969), 66.

2. Le Sueur, *Historia,* p. 15. Martin Fernandez Navarreta et al., *Colección de Documentos Inéditos para la historia de España* (Madrid, 1843), vol. 3, pp. 418–447. The danger of prosecution for treason should not be discounted: a certain Martin de Guerre was hanged in Rouen in 1555 for having brought letters from Spain via Bayonne to

Spanish merchants in Rouen "highly prejudicial to us [the king] and our republic" (AN, JJ263ᵃ, 271ʳ-272ʳ). What relation, if any, this Martin de Guerre bore to our Martin Guerre is unknown.

3. Viala, _Parlement,_ p. 409. M. A. Du Bourg, _Histoire du grand-prieuré de Toulouse et des diverses possessions de l'ordre de Saint-Jean de Jérusalem dans le sud-ouest de la France_ (Toulouse, 1883), ch. 5.

4. Coras, pp. 88–89. Le Sueur, _Historia,_ p. 15; _Histoire,_ D iiʳ.

5. Coras, pp. 89–90, 149. Le Sueur, _Historia,_ p. 17; _Histoire,_ D iiiᵛ-D ivʳ. One of the hidden questions was the details about Martin Guerre's confirmation. This took place, for some reason, at Pamiers rather than at Rieux, the seat of the bishopric, or at Artigat during a visit from the bishop's vicar. A few villages in the area were part of the civil diocese of Rieux _and_ part of the spiritual diocese of Pamiers, but Artigat was not one of them; C. Barrière-Flavy, "Le Diocèse de Pamiers au seizième siècle, d'après les procès-verbaux de 1551," _Revue des Pyrénées,_ 4 (1894), 85–106. Perhaps the judges thought this a very good question on which to test the prisoner, but he got the location right nonetheless.

6. Coras, pp. 97–99. Le Sueur, _Historia,_ pp. 15–16; _Histoire,_ D iiʳ⁻ᵛ. Imbert and Levasseur, _Le Pouvoir,_ pp. 166–167. B. Schnapper, "Testes inhabiles: Les Témoins reprochables dans l'ancien droit pénal," _Tijdschrift voor Rechtsgeschiedenis,_ 33 (1965), 594–604.

7. ADHG, B, La Tournelle, vol. 73, March 2 and 5, 1559/60; vol. 76, September 6, 1560. Le Sueur, _Historia,_ p. 16.

8. Coras, pp. 98–107. Le Sueur, _Historia,_ pp. 16–17; _Histoire,_ D iiᵛ-D iiiʳ.

9. These are the actual words in the register of the Parlement. ADHG, B, La Tournelle, 76, September 12, 1560.

10. Schnapper, "La Justice criminelle," table 4; "Les Peines arbitraires du XIIIᵉ au XVIIIᵉ siècle," _Tijdschrift voor Rechtsgeschiedenis,_ 42 (1974), 93–100. Soman, "Criminal Jurisprudence," pp. 50–54. Coras, pp. 111–112. Isambert, _Recueil général des anciennes lois,_ vol. 12, pp. 357–358. A. Carpentier and G. Frerejouan de Saint, _Répertoire général alphabétique du droit français_ (Paris, 1901), vol. 22, "Faux." Hélène Michaud, _La Grand Chancellerie et les écritures royales au 16ᵉ siècle_ (Paris, 1967), pp. 356–357. AN, X²ᵃ119, June 15, 1557; X²ᵃ914, June 15, 1557. ADR, BP443, 294ᵛ-296ʳ.

11. Coras, pp. 111, 118–123. La Roche-Flavin, _Arrests notables du Parlement de Tolose,_ p. 14.

12. Coras, pp. 24, 26–27, 109, 132–134. Imbert, *Practique iudiciaire*, pp. 488–490.

13. ADHG, B, La Tournelle, vol. 72, January 29, 1559/60. Imbert, *Practique iudiciaire*, p. 516. Imbert and Levasseur, *Le Pouvoir*, p. 175.

14. Coras, pp. 135–142.

15. Le Sueur, *Historia*, p. 18; *Histoire*, D iv^v–E i^r. Coras, p. 128.

16. Le Sueur, *Historia*, p. 19; *Histoire*, E i^v. E. Telle, "Montaigne et le procès Martin Guerre," *Bibliothèque d'humanisme et renaissance*, 37 (1975), 387–419. In principle, only the pronouncement of the sentence was open to the public in a criminal case; if Montaigne witnessed any earlier proceedings, it was in violation of court rules.

17. Coras, pp. 144–160. Le Sueur, *Historia*, pp. 20–22; *Histoire*, E ii^{r-v}.

10. The Storyteller

1. Coras, p. 78.

2. Le Sueur, *Historia*, title page and p. 22. Louis-Eugène de la Gorgue-Rosny, *Recherches généalogiques sur les comtés de Ponthieu, de Boulogne, de Guines et pays circonvoisins* (Paris, 1874–1877), vol. 3, pp. 1399–1400. ADPC, 9B24, 120^r–121^v. A. d'Haultefeuille and L. Bénard, *Histoire de Boulogne-sur-Mer* (Boulogne-sur-Mer, 1866), vol. 1, pp. 314–315, 377. *Dictionnaire historique et archéologique du département du Pas-de-Calais. Arrondissement de Boulogne* (Arras, 1882), vol. 1, pp. 267–269. *Les Bibliothèques françoises de La Croix du Maine et Du Verdier* (Paris, 1772), vol. 1, p. 349. *Liber qui vulgo Tertius Maccabaeorum inscribitur, Latin versibus à Graeca oratione expressus, A Gulielmo Sudorio, Caesarum apud Boloniens. Belg. patrono* (Paris: Robert II Estienne, 1566), dedication to Michel de L'Hôpital. *Antiquitez de Boulongne-sur-mer par Guillaume Le Sueur*, 1596, ed. E. Deseille, in *Mémoires de la société académique de l'arrondissement de Boulogne-sur-Mer*, 9, (1878–79), 1–212.

3. *Ioannis Corasii Tolosatis, Iurisconsulti Clarissimi, in Nobilissimum Titulum Pandectarum, De verbor. obligationibus, Scholia* (Lyon: Guillaume Rouillé, 1550). *Ioannis Corasii . . . vita: per Antonium Usilium . . . in schola Monspeliensi iuris civilis professorem, edita. 1559*, in Jean de Coras, *De iuris Arte libellus* (Lyon: Antoine Vincent, 1560). Coras

himself reported his youthful academic exploits in a letter from Padua, dated May 22, 1535, to Jacques de Minut, first president of the Parlement of Toulouse; it was printed with the hundred sentences at the end of his *Miscellaneorum Iuris Civilis, Libri Sex* (Lyon: G. Rouillé, 1552). Coras, p. 56. Henri de Mesmes, *Mémoires inédites,* ed. E. Frémy (Paris, n.d.), pp. 139–140, 143; Coras was one of de Mesme's professors at Toulouse. Jacques Gaches, *Mémoires sur les Guerres de Religion à Castres at dans le Languedoc, 1555–1610,* ed. C. Pradel (Paris, 1879), p. 117, n. 1. Jean de Coras, *Opera quae haberi possunt omnia* (Wittenberg, 1603), vol. 2, p. 892. The humanist jurist Jean de Boyssoné, former professor at Toulouse, also spoke of Coras's glory as a lecturer; Gatien Arnoult, "Cinq letters de Boysonné à Jean de Coras," *Revue historique de Tarn,* 3, (1880–1881), 180–185.

4. ADHG, B37 (arrêts civils), July 12, 1544. The name of Coras's mother is given here as Jeanne; Usilis reports it as Catherine. Jean de Coras, *In Titulum Codicis Iustiniani, De Iure Emphyteutico* (Lyon: Guillaume Rouillé, 1550), verso of title page: "Domino Ioanni Corasio patri suo observandissimo, Ioannes Corasius filius S. D.," dated Lyon, September 1549.

5. Coras, *Opera omnia,* vol. 1, pp. 549, 690. Archives Municipales de Toulouse, AA103^v; ADHG, 3E12004, 56^r (references kindly provided by Barbara B. Davis).

6. Marcel Fournier, "Cujas, Corras, Pacius. Trois conduites de professeurs de droit par les villes de Montpellier et Valence au seizième siècle," *Revue des Pyrénées,* 2 (1890), 328–334. Jean de Coras, *De Impuberum . . . Commentarii* (Toulouse: Guy Boudeville, 1541); p. 168 in the copy at the Bibliothèque Municipale de Toulouse has "Corrasissima" in the margin. The work is dedicated to Jean Bertrand, president, Parlement of Paris; *De acqui. possessione* is dedicated to Mansencal in 1542. The dedication to the Cardinal of Châtillon dates from 1548, to the Cardinal of Lorraine from 1549. Coras, *Opera Omnia,* vol. 1, pp. 22, 162, 191, 225.

7. Usilis, "Vita." IADHG, B46, f. 172.

8. ADHG, E916. These letters have been published in part by Charles Pradel, *Lettres de Coras, celles de sa femme, de son fils et de ses amis* (Albi, 1880), and studied by F. Neubert, "Zur problematik französicher Renaissancebriefe," *Bibliothèque d'humanisme et renaissance,* 26 (1964), 28–54. Gaches, *Mémoires,* p. 120, n. 2. Coras

had married Jacquette by June 1557, the date at which he wrote an affectionate dedication to Antoine de Saint-Paul, "maître des requêtes ordinaires de l'hôtel du roi," the uncle of Jacquette (*Opera omnia*, vol. 2, p. 894). Pradel, *Lettres*, p. 13, n. 1; p. 32, n. 1. IADHG, B75, f. 167.

9. *Lettres de Coras*, pp. 10, 12–13, 15, 20–21, 26–28, 35–36. ADHG, Letters of April 10, July 12 and December 8, 1567.

10. Jean de Coras, *In Universam sacerdotiorum materiam ... paraphrasis* (Paris: Arnaud l'Angelier, 1549), chapter on the Pope. Coras, *Des Mariages clandestinement et irreveremment contractes par les enfans de famille au deceu ou contre le gré, vouloir et consentement de leurs Peres et Meres, petit discours ... A trêcretien ... prince Henri deuxieme ... Roy de France* (Toulouse: Pierre du Puis, 1557), p. 92.

11. *Des mariages clandestinement ... contractes*, dedication to Henri II. *Altercacion en forme de Dialogue de l'Empereur Adrian et du Philosophe Epictéte ... rendu de Latin en François par monsieur maître Iean de Coras* (Toulouse: Antoine André, 1558); the privilege for nine years is dated April 4, 1557/58. *De iuris Arte libellus* (Lyon: Antoine Vincent, 1560). This work and the legal thought of Jean de Coras are the subject of A. London Fell, Jr., *Origins of Legislative Sovereignty and the Legislative State* (Königstein and Cambridge, Mass., 1983).

12. Jean de Coras, *Remonstrance Discourue par Monsieur Maistre Jean de Coras, Conseiller du Roy au Parlement de Tolose: sur l'installation par luy faicte de Messire Honorat de Martins et de Grille en l'estat de Seneschal de Beaucaire, Le 4 Novembre 1566 à Nymes* (Lyon: Guillaume Rouillé, 1567), pp. 17–19. G. Bosquet, *Histoire sur les troubles Advenus en la ville de Tolose l'an 1562* (Toulouse, 1595), p. 157. ADHG, B56 (auteurs civils), 117ᵛ 110ʳ, Germain La Faille, *Annales de la ville de Toulouse* (Toulouse, 1687–1701), vol. 2, pp. 220, 261. Also see my Chapter 12, especially n. 2. *Lettres de Coras*, p. 13.

13. Le Sueur, *Historia*, p. 12. Coras p. 64.

14. Coras, p. 87. Le Sueur, *Historia*, p. 14.

15. Coras *Altercacion*, pp. 59–63.

16. Coras, p. 12; Le Sueur, *Historia*, p. 18; *Histoire*, D ivʳ. Stephen Greenblatt, *Renaissance Self-Fashioning: From More to Shakespeare* (Chicago, 1980). For a somewhat different approach, see Norbert Elias, *The Civilizing Process: The Development of Manners*, tr. E. Jephcott (New York, 1977). Michel de Montaigne, *Oeuvres complètes*, ed.

Albert Thibaudet and Maurice Rat (Bibliothèque de la Pléiade; Paris, 1962), book 2, ch. 18: "Du démentir."

11. Histoire prodigieuse, Histoire tragique

1. *Admiranda historia*, verso of title page. *Histoire Admirable d'un Faux et Supposé Mary*, E iii^v, the privilege to Sertenas for six years, dated January 25, 1560/61. Jean-Pierre Seguin, *L'Information en France avant le périodique. 517 Canards imprimés entre 1529 et 1631* (Paris, n.d.); *L'Information en France de Louis XII à Henri II* (Geneva, 1961).

2. E. Droz, "Antoine Vincent: La Propagande protestante par le Psautier," in *Aspects de la propagande religieuse, études publiées par G. Berthoud et al.* (Geneva, 1957), pp. 276–293. N. Z. Davis, "Le Monde de l'imprimerie humaniste: Lyon," in *Histoire de l'édition française*, ed. Henri-Jean Martin and Roger Chartier (Paris, 1982), vol. 1, pp. 255–277.

3. Seguin, *L'Information . . . de Louis XII à Henri II*, reign of François I: nos. 55, 142; reign of Henri II: no. 29. Jean Papon, *Recueil d'arrestz notables des courts souveraines de France* (Lyon: Jean de Tournes, 1557).

4. Jean Céard, *La Nature et les prodiges: L'Insolite au XVIe siècle en France* (Geneva, 1977), pp. 252–265. Michel Simonin, "Notes sur Pierre Boaistuau," *Bibliothèque d'humanisme et renaissance*, 38 (1976), 323–333. Seguin, *L'information . . . de Louis XII à Henri II*, reign of Henri II: no., 22. Pierre Boaistuau, *Histoires prodigieuses les plus memorables qui ayent esté observées depuis la Nativité de Iesus Christ iusques à nostre siècle* (Paris: Vincent Sertenas, 1560). Jean de Tournes had published *Des prodiges* of Jules Obsequent in 1555, five years before the *Admiranda historia* of Guillaume Le Sueur. Le Sueur, *Histoire*, verso of title page. Coras, pp. 11–12.

5. Coras, p. 1.

6. Coras, pp. 2–7, 40–45, 118–123.

7. Coras, pp. 44–45, 96.

8. Antoine Vincent's privilege for the Psalter is dated October 19, 1561. On Jean de Monluc, see AN, MM249, 130^v–133^r, 136^{r-v}, and Vidal, *Schisme et hérésie*, pp. 165–166. "Projet d'ordonnance sur les mariages," in Calvin, *Opera omnia*, vol. 38, pp. 35–44.

9. Coras, *Arrest Memorable* (1561), f.* 2^{r-v}. I am grateful to Annie Charon for information about the Catholic ties of Vincent Sertenas and the Parisian publishers of Coras's *Arrest Memorable*.

10. Le Sueur, *Historia*, pp. 11, 18. Coras, pp. 90, 108–109, 123–128. ADHG, B, La Tournelle, vol. 74, May 20, 1560; vol. 76, September 12, 1560.

11. Coras, pp. 11–22, 139, 149.

12. *Cent Nouvelles Nouvelles*, conte 35. Compare the *Heptaméron* of Marguerite de Navarre, Second Day, conte 14 (the Sire de Bonnivet substitutes for the Italian lover of a Milanese woman); Fifth Day, conte 48 (two Franciscans substitute for the new husband of a village bride in Périgord); Shakespeare's *All's Well That Ends Well* (Helen substitutes for Diana in the tryst with Bertram, Count of Roussillon), and *Measure for Measure* (Mariana substitutes for Isabelle in the tryst with Angelo). In all of these the tricked person learns the truth only when it is revealed to her or him later. Stith Thompson gives no reference to a tale with the same type of imposture as that in the story of Martin Guerre; the closest example is a twin who deceives the wife of his brother; *Motif-Index of Folk Literature* (Bloomington, 1955–1958), K1915–1917, K1311.

13. Vladimir Propp, *Morphologie du conte*, tr. Marguerite Derrida (Paris, 1970).

14. Coras, *Arrest Memorable* (1561), f.** 3^{r-v}, pp. 70–71.

15. Coras, *Arrest Memorable* (Lyon: Antoine Vincent, 1565), pp. 158–178, annotation 104. Coras (1572), f. *ii^{r-v}. Le Sueur, *Historia*, pp. 4, 11, 22; *Histoire*, A iii^{i}, C iii^{v}. Henry C. Lancaster, *The French Tragi-Comedy: Its Origin and Development from 1552 to 1628* (Baltimore, 1907); Marvin T. Herrick, *Tragicomedy: Its Origin and Development in Italy, France and England* (Urbana, 1955); Susan Snyder, *The Comic Matrix of Shakespeare's Tragedies* (Princeton, 1979).

16. *Histoires tragiques, Extraictes des oeuvres Italiennes de Bandel, et mises en langue Françoise: Les six premieres, par Pierre Boaistuau . . . Et les suivantes par François de Belleforest* (Paris, 1580); Richard A. Carr, *Pierre Boaistuau's "Histoires Tragiques": A Study of Narrative Form and Tragic Vision* (Chapel Hill, 1979); Coras, p. 147.

17. Coras, pp. 107, 138. *Lettres de Coras*, p. 16. The self-fashioning Bertrande does not appear in Le Sueur's text.

12. Of the Lame

1. ADHG, E916, December 8, 1567. A Latin inscription on the flyleaf of the 1579 edition at the Bibliothèque de l'Arsenal says the copy was bought for 10 sous in February 1583, a middling price for a book of this kind.

2. ADHG, B56 (arrêts civils), 557^v–558^r; B57, 65^r, 70^r–73^v; B67, 478^v–479^r. IADHG, B64, f. 69; B62, f. 73; B68, f. 449. Archives Municipales de Toulouse, GG826, deposition of May 26, 1562 (reference kindly provided by Joan Davies). [Jean de Coras?], *Les Iniquitez, Abus, Nullitez, Iniustices, oppressions et Tyrannies de l'Arrest donné au Parlement de Toloze, contre les Conseillers de la Religion,* February 1568, in *Histoire de Nostre Temps, Contenant un Recueil des Choses Memorables passees et publiees pour le faict de la Religion et estat de la France, depuis l'Edict de pacification du 23 iour de Mars 1568 iusques au iour present. Imprimé Nouvellement. Mil D. LXX* [La Rochelle: Barthélemy Berton], pp. 321–354. E. Droz, *Barthélemy Berton, 1563–1573* (*L'Imprimerie à La Rochelle,* 1; Geneva, 1960), pp. 98–106. J. de Galle, "Le Conseil de la Reine de Navarre à La Rochelle . . . 1569–70," *Bulletin de la société de l'histoire du protestantisme français,* 2 (1855), 123–137. *Lettres de Coras,* pp. 23–28. Jacques Gaches, *Mémoires,* pp. 75, 117–120, 193, 417–418. The third judge slain by the crowd was Antoine I de Lacger, older brother of Antoine II de Lacger, the husband of Coras's daughter Jeanne.

3. See my bibliography on these editions. The copy of the Latin edition, Frankfurt, 1576, at the Bibliothèque Nationale (F32609) bears the signature of the seventeenth-century English collector Kenelme Digby.

4. Examples of the *Arrest Memorable* in the possession of lawyers: 1561, Bibliothèque Municipale de Lille; Lyon, 1565, Bibliothèque Municipale de Poitiers. Copies bound with *Paraphraze sur l'Edict des mariages clandestinement contractez,* Paris, 1572: Bibliothèque Nationale (F32604); Bibliothèque Municipale de Lyon (337624); Paris, 1579; Robinson Collection, Faculty of Law, University of California, Berkeley. Copies bound with other works on marriage law: Lyon, 1565, British Library, original owner French (G 19.341); Lyon, 1605, Saint Geneviève. The edition of 1561 bound with the *Ad-*

miranda historia of Le Sueur is at the Bibliothèque Nationale (F13876) and bears the signature of the great booklover Claude Dupuys.

5. See my bibliography.

6. Jean Papon, *Recueil d'Arrests Notables des Courts souveraines de France* (Paris: Nicolas Chesneau, 1565), 452ᵛ–456ᵛ. Géraud de Maynard, *Notables et singulieres Questions du Droict Escrit* (Paris, 1623), pp. 500–507; C. Drouhet, *Le poète François Mainard (1583?–1646).* (Paris, n.d.), pp. 7–8. Pasquier, *Recherches de la France,* book 6, ch. 35.

7. Herodotus, *Historiae libri IX et de vita Homeri libellus . . . Apologia Henr. Stephani pro Herodoto* (Geneva: Henri Estienne, 1566), f.**** iiʳ. Henri Estienne, *L'Introduction au traité de la conformité des merveilles anciennes avec les modernes* (1566), ed. P. Ristelhuber (Paris, 1879), pp. 24–25. Gilbert Cousin, *Narrationum sylva qua Magna Rerum* (Basel, 1567), book 8. Antoine Du Verdier, *Les Diverses Lecons* (Lyon: Barthélemy Honorat, 1577), book 4, chs. 21–27. *Histoires prodigieuses, extraictes de plusiers fameux Autheurs . . . divisees en deux Tomes. Le premier mis en lumiere par P. Boaistuau . . . Le second par Claude de Tesserant, et augmenté de dix histoires par François de Belle-Forest Comingeois* (Paris: Jean de Bordeaux, 1574), vol. 2, ff. 279ʳ–289ʳ. *Cosmographie universelle . . . enrichie par François de Belle-forrest,* p. 372. Céard, *Les Prodiges,* pp. 326–335.

8. Papon, 456ʳ⁻ᵛ; Du Verdier, pp. 300–301; Pasquier, pp. 570–571. Alfred Soman, "La Sorcellerie vue du Parlement de Paris au début du XVIIᵉ siècle," in *La Gironde de 1601 à nos jours. Questions diverses. Actes du 104ᵉ Congrès national des Sociétés Savantes, Bordeaux, 1979* (Paris, 1981), pp. 393–405.

9. Auger Gaillard, *Oeuvres complètes,* publ. and tr. Ernest Nègre (Paris, 1970), pp. 514, 525–526.

10. Montaigne, *Oeuvres complètes,* book 3, ch. 11. I use John Florio's contemporary translation, *The Essayes or Morall, Politike and Millitarie Discourses of Lord Michael de Montaigne* (London, 1610), "Of the Lame or Cripple," pp. 612–617.

11. Coras, pp. 52, 74, 88. Montaigne, *Essayes,* pp. 614, 616. *Quinti Horatii Flacci Emblemata* (Antwerp: Philippe Lisaert, 1612), pp. 180–181: "Rarò antecedentem scelestum / Deseruit pede poena claudo," from the *Odes,* book 3, ode 2. Cesare Ripa, *Iconologia overo*

Descrittione dell'Imagini universali cavate dall'Antichità et da Altri Luoghi (Rome: Heirs Gio. Gigliotti, 1593), p. 37: Bugia. The personification of Lying has a wooden leg because "la bugia ha le gambe corte." Other examples of mixed meanings of a wooden leg or lameness: Saturn with a wooden leg (Adhémar, *Inventaire*, vol. 2, p. 272); lameness or deformity of the feet associated with straying from divine truth and with iniquity (Giovanni Piero Valeriano Bolzoni, *Hieroglyphica* [Lyon: Paul Frellon, 1602], pp. 366–367).

Epilogue

1. ADAr, 5E6653, 63^r, 97^r–98^r. Coras, pp. 23–24.

2. F. Pasquier, "Coutumes du Fossat," pp. 278–320. Philippe Wolff, *Regards sur le midi médiéval* (Toulouse, 1978), pp. 412–414.

3. François Rabelais, *Oeuvres*, ed. J. Boulanger (Bibliothèque de la Pléiade, Paris, 1955), *Pantagruel*, prologue, p. 169. This saying is current in Languedoc today. F. Mistral, *Lou Tresor dóu Felibrige ou Dictionnaire Provençal-Français* (Aix-en-Provence, 1979), II, 302.

4. ADHG, B, Insinuations, vol. 6, 95^v–97^v. Only Pierre *le jeune* is described as the son of Martin Guerre's widow, Jehanne Carolle. He is still a minor with two "curateurs," which suggests that he is between fifteen and twenty-five years of age, and he lives with his mother. The Carol family (also Carrel, Carolz) were from Artigat, though of less high status than the Rols (ADAr, 5E6656, 9^r).

5. ACArt, register of marriages and baptisms of the parish of Artigat, 1632–1642. Terrier of 1651: Dominique Guerre; Gaspard Guerre, alias Bonnelle; Ramond Guerre; Jean Guerre; Jammes Guerre, François Guerre, and Martin Guerre, brothers; the heirs of Marie Guerre. Pierre Rols holds several fields in common with the heirs of Marie Guerre. The Guerres of Artigat survived their trials more easily than the Daguerres of Hendaye survived the witchcraft prosecutions in the Labourd in 1609. Marie and Johannes Daguerre were among those testifying, and Petri Daguerre, aged seventy-three, was described by the judge from Bordeaux as "the master of ceremonies and governor of the sabbath" and was executed. There were still Daguerres in Hendaye in 1620, one fairly prominent though not a village *jurat* (de Lancre, *Tableau de l'inconstance*, pp. 71, 125, 217;

ADPyA, 1J160, no. 46, Jan. 14, 1620). The du Tilhs continued in Sajas and Le Pin in the seventeenth and eighteenth centuries, but their status was still modest (ADHG, 2E2403, 43^v–45^r, 4E2016).

6. ACArt, Register of Baptisms, 1634: "born a bastard ... Jean, son of Ramond Guerre." Quite a few immigrant workers to Spain set up a second family there, to return later to their wife and children in Languedoc (oral communication from Jean-Pierre Poussou).

Index